ADVANCE PRAISE

Trudy uses her most challenging life lessons to magnify the faithfulness of God. Readers will be encouraged by the relatable stories and challenged to withstand, climb, and overcome the mountains of adversity they face in their own lives.

Andy Stanley, Atlanta, GA
Author, Communicator, and Founder
of North Point Ministries

No matter who we are or where we're from, we all face mountains, or challenges, in life. Trudy opens her life to share some of her biggest challenges while also reminding us that the presence and power of God is bigger than even our biggest challenge. This book will inspire you to keep climbing your mountains through the power of God's Spirit in you.

Christine Caine
Bestselling author, Founder of
A21 and Propel Women

Trudy Cathy White is a beautiful mountain climber. With a trial-tested and wise voice, she gives us a guide to scale life's steepest mountains, led by confidence in the faithfulness and goodness of God. Climb Every Mountain *is a vital resource for the journey of life, and I'm grateful for the way Trudy shares from her wealth of experience and obedience to our Savior. Keep this book close by!*

Shelley Giglio, Atlanta, GA
Chief Strategist, sixstepsrecords
Co-founder, Passion Conferences/
Choice Ministries

When I was in high school, there was a sign in our locker room that read, "When the going gets tough, the tough get going." That saying really impacted my life and became my mantra for dealing with difficult times. I'll have to admit, it didn't always work until my belief in Jesus became central in my life and I modified the statement to read, "When the going gets tough, the Lord is always by our side." Read Trudy Cathy White's wonderful book Climb Every Mountain and learn the truth of this statement many times over. Thanks, Trudy!

Ken Blanchard, Escondido, CA
Co-founder and Chief Spiritual Officer
of The Ken Blanchard Companies

Trudy Cathy White's book is disarmingly simple and helpful. She chooses a series of "mountains" that Christians must all climb as they seek to live lives of service to God. These range from stewarding wealth to raising children to facing tragedy. She lays out a pathway up each mountain with three questions about "Know, Be, Live"— what must I know, who must I become, and what practical things should I do, in order to climb this mountain? Her counsel is personal, practical, and always accessible. An enjoyable read!

Tim Keller
Pastor Emeritus, Redeemer
Presbyterian Church

Climb Every
MOUNTAIN

Climb Every MOUNTAIN

FINDING GOD FAITHFUL
IN THE JOURNEY OF LIFE

TRUDY CATHY WHITE

Written in collaboration with ECHO Creative Media (Dawn Sherill-Porter and Brenda Noel) and Allen Harris.

Unless otherwise noted, Scripture quotations are taken from the Holy Bible, New International Version®, NIV®. Copyright © 1973, 1978, 1984, 2011 by Biblica, Inc.™ Used by permission of Zondervan. All rights reserved worldwide. www.zondervan.com The "NIV" and "New International Version" are trademarks registered in the United States Patent and Trademark Office by Biblica, Inc.™

Scripture quotations designated (ESV) are taken from The Holy Bible, English Standard Version®, copyright © 2001 by Crossway, a publishing ministry of Good News Publishers. Used by permission. All rights reserved.

Scripture quotations designated (NKJV) are taken from the New King James Version®. Copyright © 1982 by Thomas Nelson. Used by permission. All rights reserved.

Scripture quotations marked (NLT) are taken from the Holy Bible, New Living Translation, copyright ©1996, 2004, 2007, 2013, 2015 by Tyndale House Foundation. Used by permission of Tyndale House Publishers, Inc., Carol Stream, Illinois 60188. All rights reserved.

Scripture quotations marked (CEV) are taken from the Contemporary English Version, copyright © 1991, 1992, 1995 by American Bible Society. Used by Permission. All Rights Reserved.

Scripture quotations marked (MSG) are taken from *THE MESSAGE*, copyright © 1993, 1994, 1995, 1996, 2000, 2001, 2002 by Eugene H. Peterson. Used by permission of NavPress. All rights reserved. Represented by Tyndale House Publishers, Inc.

Scripture quotations marked (NASB) are taken from the New American Standard Bible® (NASB), Copyright © 1960, 1962, 1963, 1968, 1971, 1972, 1973, 1975, 1977, 1995 by The Lockman Foundation. Used by permission. www.Lockman.org

ISBN: 9781948677127
ISBN: 9781948677134 (eBook)

Cover Design by Bruce Gore, Gore Studio
Interior design by Bill Kersey, KerseyGraphics

TABLE OF CONTENTS

FOREWORD. *10*

Miss Johnnie Armstrong

INTRODUCTION *18*

In the last days the mountain of the LORD's temple will be established as the highest of the mountains; it will be exalted above the hills, and peoples will stream to it. —MICAH 4:1

CHAPTER 1
CALLED BY NAME TO CLIMB 22

I have summoned you by name; you are mine. —ISAIAH 43:1

CHAPTER 2
MANAGING GOD'S GIFT OF GRACE ON THE JOURNEY . *38*

Each of you should use whatever gift you have received to serve others, as faithful stewards of God's grace in its various forms. —1 PETER 4:10

CHAPTER 3
SCALING TOWARD SIGNIFICANCE 60

By the grace of God I am what I am. —1 CORINTHIANS 15:10 (NLT)

CHAPTER 4

BUILDING A FIRM FOUNDATION *76*

Train up a child in the way he should go, and when he is old he will not depart from it. –PROVERBS 22:6 (NKJV)

CHAPTER 5

BLAZING A TRAIL FOR OTHERS TO FOLLOW *94*

Your testimonies are my heritage forever, for they are the joy of my heart. –PSALM 119:111 (ESV)

CHAPTER 6

TRIALS OF THE TRAIL *112*

Cast your cares on the LORD and he will sustain you. –PSALM 55:22

CHAPTER 7

STRENGTH TO SUMMIT *130*

Even to your old age and gray hairs I am he, I am he who will sustain you. –ISAIAH 46:4

CHAPTER 8

ANCHORED SECURELY *146*

*When you pass through the waters, I will be with you;
and when you pass through the rivers, they will not sweep
over you. When you walk through the fire, you will not be
burned; the flames will not set you ablaze.* –ISAIAH 43:2

CHAPTER 9

LET US GO UP TO THE MOUNTAIN *164*

*I lift up my eyes to the mountains—where does my
help come from? My help comes from the LORD, the
Maker of heaven and earth.* –PSALM 121:1–2

AFTERWORD: CLIMB ON! *184*

*Who am I, Sovereign LORD, and what is my family, that
you have brought me this far?* –2 SAMUEL 7:18

ACKNOWLEDGMENTS. *188*

Foreword

Dear Reader,

I first met Trudy Cathy in the summer of 1964 when she attended her very first summer camp at Camp Crestridge for Girls. I recall welcoming a vivacious little girl who was beyond excited for her first camp experience. At the time, I served as the assistant director for Camp Crestridge and had ample opportunity to get to know Trudy as I directed various activities.

One of those activities was a weekly event known as "Campfire." Campfire evenings started with campers building a fire and preparing their dinners outside their cabins; dinner was immediately followed by an evening walk through the beautiful North Carolina woods to an outdoor amphitheater. With music playing from the nearby chapel porch and campers placed on a "talking ban," we walked the narrow gravel path toward our destination. We felt dwarfed by the mountains that rose majestically all around us.

When we arrived at the amphitheater, campers and counselors gathered around a large bonfire with a spectacular view of the lake and the mountains just beyond. In this peaceful setting, it was my responsibility to challenge and encourage the faith of the campers. Some of my sweetest memories of camp arise from times spent with the glow of the flames illuminating expectant, young faces.

Trudy was present during one of those "Campfire" nights when I felt led to turn the campers' gazes across the lake and to the mountains in front of them.

An evening fog had begun to descend over our gathering, obscuring the world outside the glow of the bonfire. Asking the campers to look around us, I inquired who among them could see the gigantic, looming mountains that had been clearly visible when we had gathered in this same place just the week before. Not a single camper raised her hand. "But which of you still believe they exist?" Every hand in the amphitheater quickly shot into the air.

GOD IS OUR REFUGE AND STRENGTH.

"You see," I began, "our God, like these mountains, can't always be seen. Yet as big and steadfast as these mountains appear, God is much more powerful, faithful, and constant." I don't specifically remember Trudy's face in the crowd of young girls as I gave this message, but I'm told it was one of the moments she first understood the Lord's present help in time of need (Psalm 46:1, "God is our refuge and strength, an ever-present help in trouble."). I was not aware until much later that this teaching began a lifelong guiding principle for Trudy; significant events of her life became mountain-themed moments.

In her ten years at camp, eight years as a camper and two years as a junior counselor, I watched Trudy's character grow as she learned of the faithfulness of the Lord and put her trust in Him. The day came when Trudy grew up and left her camp experiences in the past. However, she and I stayed in touch after she outgrew our camp program.

I was thrilled to hear of her accomplishments as a student, marriage to John, and joy of becoming a mother. My heart soared as she and John made the decision to follow the Lord's leading to further His kingdom as missionaries to Brazil.

A few years after John and Trudy's return stateside, Trudy called me with exciting news. I heard great anticipation, worry, and thrill in her voice as she shared the opportunity to serve as interim director of WinShape Camps for Girls. "Miss Johnnie," she said, "I've never been a camp director before, but you have! Would you share wisdom from your years of experience?" I was overjoyed to hear a former camper had been so impacted by her time at camp that she wished to create that same environment for other young girls.

I shared what knowledge I had gained knowing full well the woman at the other end of the phone would not only succeed in this new endeavor, but thrive. Trudy's servant heart and passion to shape the lives of young women enlivened the girl's program at WinShape Camps; ultimately, the WinShape Foundation insisted she serve as permanent director. Trudy served in this capacity for thirteen tremendous years.

When I think of Trudy, my mind goes to James 1:4. The author states it is our steadfastness in trials which make us complete, lacking in nothing. Many would say Trudy is "lacking in nothing" in reference to her position in life; however, Trudy's true "completeness" is a faith made strong through steadfast pursuit of the Lord as she faces life's most difficult challenges. I am consistently challenged by the depth of Trudy's faith in her heavenly Father; her life embodies the presence of Christ as she faces each storm with genuine peace, looking to her Lord for guidance.

A few weeks back, I saw Trudy's name pop up on my phone, as it generally does every few months. My heart leapt in anticipation of talking to my dear friend. However, I was ill prepared for the conversation that followed. Trudy explained she was working on a second book about climbing life's mountains with care and confidence in God. After encapsulating what you will soon glean from the pages of this book, Trudy moved on to the real reason she had called—she requested that I write the foreword.

Trudy's request was one of the most unexpected and beautiful blessings of my eighty-five years. To know I have had even the smallest of impacts on her life warms my heart and fills me with a sense of great fulfillment. The Lord has been so good to me; He has seen me through the darkest of valleys and greatest of joys! I'm incredibly blessed to consider Trudy a friend, sister in Christ, and an example of steadfast faith to follow.

I pray the Lord's infinite wisdom would speak to each of you through the words Trudy has written. Prepare your hearts to receive from this incredible woman of God.

Love you dear,
Miss Johnnie

ASSOCIATE PROFESSOR OF PHYSICAL
EDUCATION, BLUE MOUNTAIN COLLEGE
COORDINATOR OF THE DEGREE
PROGRAM IN PHYSICAL EDUCATION

Johnnie Armstrong has served for over sixty-three years at Blue Mountain College. She graduated from BMC in 1953 and returned a year later to start up and guide the college's athletics teams. Johnnie was the first Athletics Director and women's basketball coach at the college. She was instrumental in establishing its Physical Education degree and went on to become Associate Professor of Physical Education and Coordinator of the Physical Education Degree program. She was awarded an honorary doctorate in 2006.

At Camp Crestridge for Girls, Johnnie was land sports director in 1955, program director in 1956, assistant camp director in 1957, and became summer director in 1979. Following her tenure as summer director, Johnnie has returned to camp for a couple of weeks each summer, leading campfires and helping around the camp.

Introduction

***

In the last days the mountain of the Lord's temple will be
established as the highest of the mountains; it will be exalted
above the hills, and peoples will stream to it.

–MICAH 4:1

Every key moment of my life has been marked by a mountain. I'm not talking about a peak far off in the distance that simply provides beautiful background scenery. No, these mountains have been under my feet. Supporting me. Challenging me. Lifting me. Changing my perspective. Leading me ever upward and onward. I am who, what, and where I am today because *this* is where all those mountains have brought me. So as I thought about writing a second book, it only seemed fitting that I should craft it around this theme that has played such an important role in my life.

My childhood home sat beside a mountain—at least through the eyes of a little girl. Looking back, I'll admit it was more of a large hill, but it seemed so steep and regal back then. My family even called it a mountain. We'd climb to the top as a family, and then we'd sing songs, read the Bible, have picnics, watch planes fly overhead, and count the stars. Those days on our family mountain were precious to me—so precious, in fact, that my husband and I built our own home right on the top of that little mountain.

Camp Crestridge for Girls is surrounded by the beautiful North Carolina mountains. I attended summer camp there every year beginning in 1964, when I was eight years old. It was there that I learned our God is like those mountains—He is always with me and will never leave me. I gained the highest camp rank during my final summer there as a camper. It wasn't an easy process, and it included a difficult climb up Rattlesnake Mountain. The rocky summit is the highest point in the area. I worked hard to reach the top, but every cut, bruise, scrape, and blister was worth it when I got there. The view took my breath away. The process of facing, challenging, and conquering that mountain brought new meaning to the song "Climb Every Mountain" from the movie *The Sound of Music*. We sang that song every summer at the end of camp. It still gives me goosebumps whenever I hear it.

As you'll read in this book, my husband and I spent ten years as missionaries in Brazil, which is literally surrounded by mountains. Our children were young then—two of them, in fact, were born there—and one of our favorite family activities was riding the lift up Rio's famous Sugarloaf Mountain. The view from the top encompasses the beaches, forests, and neighboring mountains in majestic splendor. Whenever I got lost traveling through our home city of Rio de Janeiro (which was often), Sugarloaf Mountain was my anchor. It was the landmark I looked for as I tried to figure out in which direction I was supposed to be going.

Our youngest son spent twenty-four days in a special NICU clinic in Rio de Janeiro. As we made the bumpy ambulance ride from the hospital to the clinic shortly after his difficult delivery, it dawned on me that we were traveling *up*. The NICU, where God worked miracles to save our baby, was fixed firmly on the side of a mountain. As we spent weeks worrying about and praying for our son, the glorious view from every window in the clinic gave us endless reminders of God's enduring faithfulness and presence.

My daughter Angela and I volunteered at WinShape Camps for Girls in Mount Berry, Georgia, in the summer of 2003. As the campers gathered, I looked across at the Appalachian mountain range. God used His beautiful creation to speak to me about being involved in camps to impact the lives of young girls—a decision that has shaped the latter part of my life. In 2011, a second overnight campus for WinShape Camps for Girls was launched in Young Harris, Georgia, in the shadow of Brasstown Bald, the tallest mountain in Georgia. This became such a special place that my husband and I built a cabin there—a place of respite and retreat where much of this book was written.

I could go on and on about the importance mountains have held throughout my life. Over the years, I've come to view them in two distinct ways. First, I see mountains as symbols of God's unchanging, resolute presence. He sits like a mighty mountain, unmoving and unaffected by the storms of life. Second, mountains represent the many struggles, obstacles, and challenges I've faced throughout my life. They mark where the road gets rough, where the climb seems too steep. Some may see these dual views of mountains as contradictory. I can understand that. I suppose it's hard for some to see mountains both as a sign of God's presence *and* as a symbol of life's hardest moments. After all, God's supposed to make our lives *easy*, right? Wrong.

Life is hard. If God had intended for my days on earth to be easy, they would be. But He designed my days to be full of tools for refinement, opportunities to build character, and instruments to strengthen my resolve and trust in Him. I am challenged by my loving Father to climb onward and upward, facing every mountain with care and confidence in Him. I have no trouble seeing God *and*

LIFE IS HARD. IF GOD HAD INTENDED FOR MY DAYS ON EARTH TO BE EASY, THEY WOULD BE.

---

adversity as mountains in my life. The truth is, I've never faced a mountain of trouble where God wasn't with me already. He never sends us up a mountain alone.

Throughout this book, I want to take a journey with you. I want to embark on an expedition toward, up, and over the mountains most of us face in life. We'll tackle mountains such as figuring out our identity in Christ, learning how to make the most of the gifts He's given us, and discovering how to learn what He's calling us to do. We'll climb through the challenges of parenting and leaving (and living) a legacy for others to follow. We'll bear down and talk about what happens when adversity makes the trail too hard to tread. We'll look further down the path toward the mountains of getting older and facing grief. And as we travel together, I'll reveal the mountain-climbing principles God has taught me throughout my life by sharing some very personal stories about the mountains I've faced over the past sixty-something years.

Each chapter of this book will give you an opportunity to stop and reflect on what we're discussing. You'll be asked to spend some time in prayer and Bible study as you examine the mountains in your own life and learn how to equip yourself for the climb ahead. We'll do this through the Know–Be–Live model. First, you'll have a chance to think about the truths presented in the chapter (Know). Then, you'll take a moment to allow those truths to sink into your spirit and examine how those truths will change you (Be). Last, you'll set some specific goals and action steps for putting those truths into action (Live). Through this process, it is my prayer that you will come to Know Jesus more deeply, Be transformed in character, and Live a life of kingdom influence.

The road ahead won't always be easy—but you already know that, don't you? Since we know the mountains are looming anyway, let's lace up our hiking boots and charge up the mountain together.

CHAPTER 1

Called by Name to Climb

❧

I have summoned you by name; you are mine.
—ISAIAH 43:1

"Say hello to Mrs. Trudy! Do you know who she is? She's Truett Cathy's daughter—and he invented Chick-fil-A!"

As the former director of WinShape Camps for Girls, I've heard countless parents introduce me to their daughters that way. Of all the things I've done and all the things I am, that's always been the first thing people think of when they meet me. Some grown women may be annoyed to still be known mainly because of their father, but it's never bothered me. I'm the only woman in the whole world who's ever been known as "Truett's daughter." I loved my father. He was an amazing man, and being known as his little girl is a distinction I wear with honor. As grateful as I am to my father, though, "Truett's daughter" is just one piece of me. If you really want to know who I am, you have to dig a little deeper.

That's true of all of us, in fact. Too often, we identify ourselves as one thing. We focus on one role, job, title, event, or personality quirk and then build our entire identity around that one thing. The problem is, no matter what that one thing is, it's not enough. Without even meeting you, I already know you are more than any one trait—just as a tree is much more than a single leaf. If you really want to know me—and become known yourself—you must broaden your perspective. You have to back up and take the whole picture in, every beautiful facet.

Throughout this book, we're going to take a journey together. We're standing at the base of the mountain looking up at the amazing, challenging, wonderful, and intimidating climb ahead. Every twist and turn along the way has rich meaning, and every step is significant. And as we start the climb together, we must ask ourselves the first key question: *Who am I?*

WHO (AND WHAT) AM I?

I am many things—and so are you. Where we come from, how we've lived, and the choices we've made all work together to weave the beautiful tapestry of our lives. Seeing that big picture can be hard to do if you're used to identifying yourself by one thing, so let me give you a tip: for now, stop trying to answer the question, *Who am I?* Instead, break it down into its different parts by asking *What am I?* Asking *who* is a loaded question; it comes with a lot of pressure, as though we have to sum up our entire identity in just a few words. Answering *what* is easier, because we can all think of the different titles we have and the roles we play. For example, let me tell you a few things that I am.

I AM A DAUGHTER, SISTER, AND CHILD OF GOD

I grew up on a country farm south of Atlanta, Georgia, with my parents and two older brothers. Even as my parents built the family business, they were committed to giving us a simple, normal life. I spent my days riding ponies, climbing trees, gathering pine cones, doing chores, and enjoying the wonders of life on a farm. Since we lived out in the country, we didn't have many neighbors, which meant there weren't any other little girls nearby to play with. As a result, I knocked around with my brothers Dan and Bubba every day, horseplaying and roughhousing like one of the boys. I remember one time when I was really young—maybe four years old—when Dan told me I wouldn't be a boy when I grew up. I cried! It's not that I *wanted* to be a boy; I just didn't know who I'd be if I didn't grow up to be like my brothers. They were always there for me, taking care of their little sister and including me in their games. They were such strong role models for me, and I wanted to be just like them.

The three of us were blessed with amazing parents. Mom and Dad went out of their way to teach us about the Lord by modeling the love of Jesus in our home. They taught us from a young age the power of John 3:16, "For God so loved the world that he gave his one and only Son, that whoever believes in him shall not perish but have eternal life." I accepted Jesus as my Lord and Savior at age seven. It was easy for me to imagine a loving and forgiving heavenly Father, because my earthly father showed me his love each and every day. Don't get me wrong, though. It wasn't wall-to-wall Bible studies, strict rules, and worship songs in the Cathy home; we had fun! My parents showed us that a life lived with and for Christ doesn't have to be stuffy, boring, or restrictive. Instead, they demonstrated the unbelievable joy and truly abundant life that is found in Jesus Christ. So if you're wondering who and what I am, here are the first, fundamental pieces: I am a daughter, a sister, and, most importantly, a child of God.

I AM A WIFE, MOTHER, AND GRANDMOTHER

When I was about thirteen, my father and I were walking along the ocean at the beach. Out of the blue, he turned to me and said, "So, Trudy, what kind of guy do you want to marry some day?" I hardly knew how to respond because I hadn't yet given it much thought. Dad encouraged me to start thinking about it. He suggested I pray about it and start making a list of the kind of qualities I wanted to find in a husband. I made my list and tucked it into my Bible. I pulled it out often, updating and editing it as I matured and as God put a new vision of my ideal spouse on my heart.

Over those years, I prayed for my future husband and children. Of all the things I could become later in life, nothing excited me more than the dream of being a wife and mother. That dream was so important to me that I even began to worry about whether or not Jesus would come back before I had a chance to start a family. Not too long after I started my "husband wish list," my pastor preached a sermon on Jesus's second coming. As we closed the service by singing the great hymn "I'll Fly Away," I remember praying anxiously, "Lord, I love you, and I want to see you. But please don't come back until I have a chance to get married and have children!"

God showed me His answer to that prayer about six years later. I had moved to Birmingham, Alabama, to start college. Once there, I managed to talk my father into letting me open my very own Chick-fil-A restaurant near the school. At age nineteen, I became Chick-fil-A's youngest Operator at that time. As proud as I was of that accomplishment—not to mention the success of my restaurant—I soon realized that God had other plans for my restaurant aspirations. He didn't just place me there to open the restaurant; He put me there to introduce me to my husband. One day when I was at work, a nice young man about my age walked in to apply for a job. Boy, was he good-looking, so I hired him! As we worked together over the next several months, my thoughts kept going back to the list my father encouraged me to write. I could tell he was kind, intelligent, caring, and that he loved the Lord. I began to realize that this man, John Wheeler White, III, was everything I had ever prayed for in a husband.

Throughout my teen years, I often prayed for God to keep me faithful as I waited for the perfect person who could live up to what I envisioned on my list. I truly wanted to marry someone who shared my faith, my values, my interests, and my dreams— someone I could marry and wholeheartedly commit to as a lifelong partner. There were times when I doubted such a man even existed. But then I met John. I knew immediately that he was a special man and that I *needed* to get to know him better. He was a busy guy, however, between work, college . . . and, of course, meeting other girls on campus. I didn't like that last part, so I did something about it. Since he technically worked for me, I was the one who set his work schedule. I *might* have scheduled him to work (with me) most Friday and Saturday nights instead of leaving his weekends free for other girls. Controlling? Maybe. Effective? Definitely. We talked nonstop during those hours at the Century Plaza Chick-fil-A. Before long, we fell in love.

There were so many things that attracted me to John—his Christian faith, strong work ethic, leadership abilities, people skills, wonderful parents, respect for others, moral convictions, passion for serving others.... I could go on and on. The main thing I loved about him, though, was that he was exactly the type of man God had put on my heart as a young girl. God knew, years before I ever even met him, that John and I would be great together. After two years of working together and getting to know each other, we were married on July 16, 1977. My "husband wish list" had taken shape right in front of me, and I started my new life with the husband I'd always prayed for.

Three years later, my lifelong dream of becoming a mother came true with the birth of our first child. We were such a sight that day! John and I lived in a tiny apartment, and my mother, John's parents, and a dear family friend were all crammed into our little living room. The "team" had given me strict instructions while I was in another room resting: whenever I felt a contraction, I had to ring a little bell. When they heard that sound, everyone noted the time and calculated how close the contractions were getting. When they got close enough, *all six of us* jumped in our cars and headed to the hospital. On that amazing spring day in 1980, our daughter came into the world. I knew immediately what her name would be: Joy. She was the answer to the prayers I had offered for more than a decade, and I knew she would be all that her name implies: our *joy,* our *delight,* and *great happiness.*

That great happiness was compounded over the next seven years with the birth of three more children. In all, we were blessed with two beautiful daughters and two wonderful sons. Our four children are now all grown and married, and they've continued to bring blessing after blessing to our lives. When I met John, I knew God had big things in store for us. What He's given us, though, is more than I ever could have imagined. As we enter this later phase of our lives, I am amazed at how faithfully God has kept His promise to bring me a big, happy family. It seems like yesterday that I was a thirteen-year-old girl walking on the beach with my father, just starting to dream about the man God had in store for me. But now I'm blessed to stand beside my husband and look out over a huge family of our four children, our four "new" children (sons- and daughters-in-law), and our fifteen grandchildren.

Being a wife and mother will always be my greatest calling. What a privilege to have raised children who love Jesus and who have chosen godly spouses. What an indescribable blessing to witness all our grandchildren being raised in loving homes with Jesus at the center. There's no doubt that children are a gift from the Lord. He masterfully created my children in His image and for His purpose, and then He lovingly *entrusted* them to me. As parents, it's our task to raise our children to become a reflection of their Creator. That's what John and I have tried to do for the past four decades. There's no doubt that my roles as a wife, mother, and grandmother are huge pieces of who and what I am. I simply wouldn't be *me* without them.

I AM A FORMER MISSIONARY

Years into our marriage, John surprised me with the news that he had been feeling a prompting toward international missions. I was stunned! I'll tell the full story later in this book, but for now, let's just say I was not prepared to leave my family, friends, home, career, and all I had ever known. Plus, the thought of moving our children to a foreign country was terrifying. In time, though, God turned my heart and I realized that He wasn't simply calling *John* into missions; he was calling *our family* into missions. I had been many things throughout my life—a daughter, sister, wife, mother, business leader. But over and above all of that, I was a child of God, and He was asking me to follow Him on a new adventure. How could I say no?

We spent ten years in Brazil ministering to its wonderful people. Those first several months were quite a culture shock for us! However, learning a new language, eating unfamiliar food in an unfamiliar environment, and being surrounded by abject poverty impacted us in ways I can never accurately explain. These people had so little, and yet their hearts were so full. There was a joy and simplicity that I'd never seen before, and I quickly fell in love with the community we were serving.

Our family grew during our ten years there too. Two of our four children were born in Brazil; they spent the first years of their lives knowing nothing about the surplus of "stuff" we have here in America. They grew up alongside the boys and girls of Brazil, giving them a much different sense of what's *normal* than they'd have had here in the States. Delivering two of our children in Brazil turned out to be quite an adventure—especially with the birth of our third child, Angela. She was born in a hospital in Rio de Janeiro. After the delivery, we barely had time to even get a good look at her before the nurses took her away to clean, weigh, and measure her. A little later, once I was settled on the maternity floor, a nurse walked in with this sweet, swaddled doll of a baby girl. John and I looked down at the gurgling darling in my arms, and we were taken with how cute she was. We were also taken with the fact that she was Chinese—and John and I weren't. They had brought us the wrong baby! After a panicked call to the nurse and a bustle of activity outside our room, our sweet little Angela finally made it into my arms.

Many things about my time as a missionary have had a lasting impact in my soul to this day—and I'm not just talking about almost bringing home the wrong daughter. As I've said in the introduction to this book, mountains have always been present during key moments in my life. From a young age, I've always looked to mountains as visible testaments to the power, majesty, and firm foundation of my heavenly Father. And nowhere is that majestic grandeur more evident than in the amazing mountain ranges I discovered during these years. Mountains were *everywhere*. Every peak seemed as sturdy and solid as Almighty God Himself, ever-present witnesses to His creative splendor. During those years in a foreign land, those mountain vistas served as a constant reminder of God's presence and glory.

Today I'm what's known as a "has been" missionary. Our time in the foreign mission field is done, but our time as missionaries will never be over. John and I brought that heart for missions back home with us, and our experiences in Brazil have shaped how we've approached every ministry opportunity we've had since. I never expected the call to missions, but now I know it's a huge piece of who and what I am.

HOW DO YOU KNOW WHO YOU REALLY ARE?

So, who and what am I *really*? I'm a passionate follower of Jesus Christ. I'm a daughter and a sister. I'm a wife, mother, and grandmother. I'm a missionary. I'm a working professional. I'm the founder and leader of several nonprofit organizations serving young girls, churches, and future leaders. I'm Truett's daughter. I'm John's wife. I'm the former director of WinShape Camps for Girls. I'm an author and a speaker. I'm an entrepreneur. I was one of the youngest Operators in Chick-fil-A history. I'm a church planter. So, seriously . . . *who I am?*

The truth is, I'm *all* these things. As I said before, asking *who* is a loaded question. How can you possibly sum up everything you are, everything you've done, and everything you've experienced in one simple answer? You can't. That's why I suggested focusing on *what* you are, on the roles you play and on the things you spend time on. That's where your passions and priorities really come into focus. People often have some grand ideal in their heads about who they are, but the fact is, they're usually wrong. If you really want to know who and what you are, take a look at your calendar and your checkbook. How you spend your time and money does more to show the world who and what you are than anything else. If *who* you say you are doesn't line up with *what* you're actually doing, then you've got some more thinking to do.

If that sounds harsh or if you aren't happy with what you're discovering about yourself, I have good news. We're asking the wrong questions—or at least we aren't asking the *key* question yet. *Who* and *what* can only take you so far. They tell you things *about* yourself; they can't tell you what's really at your core. If you truly want to know who you are, you must first discover *whose* you are.

WHOSE AM I?

My mother was a wonderful and wise woman. In my decades as a parent, I have always tried to live up to the fine example she set for me. There's one memory in particular that has always stood out to me, especially in times when I get confused about who I am and what I'm supposed to do. Whenever my brothers or I would leave the house as children and teenagers, Mom stood at the door, said goodbye, and then gave us this challenge, no matter where we were going or who we were going out with: "Remember *who* you are— and *whose* you are."

Those words have echoed in my ears throughout my entire life. As I've raised my own children and worked with other children at camp, I've always encouraged them to focus less on what they want to do and more on who they need to become. To live a life of success and significance, it is imperative that we practice integrity, exercise self-discipline, make healthy life choices, develop a good work ethic, and value others more than ourselves. That describes the kind of people we all like to be around, doesn't it? However, something important—the key ingredient—is missing. After all, we don't want to simply rack up a list of *good characteristics*; we want to be men and women of *good character*. And I believe we are our best selves when we surrender fully to the love and presence of Jesus Christ in our hearts.

It is impossible for me to truly understand who I am apart from my identity in Christ. At the age of seven, I gave Jesus control of my life and I've done my best to let Him lead my actions and decisions ever since. Sure, I've messed up at times. I've turned left when He said right. I've let the desires of my

---

HOW YOU SPEND YOUR TIME AND MONEY
DOES MORE TO SHOW THE WORLD WHO AND
WHAT YOU ARE THAN ANYTHING ELSE.

---

heart lead me into painful mistakes at times. I've missed wonderful opportunities because I charged ahead on my own instead of letting Him guide me. I'm certainly not a perfect person. However, my commitment to Christ and His indwelling presence in my heart has kept me out of trouble more often than I'll ever really know. It's kept me from making some terribly unwise decisions. It has truly defined me; it's answered the question, *Who am I?* I know who I am: I am God's precious creation. I am loved by my heavenly Father and I am forgiven by the blood of His Son. I am who I am because *He* is who He is.

Whenever I doubt my self-worth, I find my value in my personal relationship with Jesus. Whenever I question my significance, I find a loving Father who cares deeply for me. When insecurities threaten, I remember Matthew 6:26, "Look at the birds of the air; they do not sow or reap or store away in barns, and yet your heavenly Father feeds them. Are you not much more valuable than they?"

When loneliness or fear loom, God brings me comfort with His presence, encouraging my heart with His Word: "Be strong and courageous. Do not be afraid or terrified because of them, for the LORD your God goes with you; He will never leave you nor forsake you" (Deuteronomy 31:6).

When I am uncertain, He reminds me that "I can do all things through Christ who strengthens me" (Philippians 4:13, NKJV).

When I find myself in times of difficulty, He sets my feet on solid ground, giving me confidence and hope to face another day. He speaks to my soul, "The Spirit himself bears witness with our spirit that we are children of God, and if children, then heirs—heirs of God and fellow heirs with Christ, provided we suffer with Him in order that we may also be glorified with Him" (Romans 8:16–17).

Who am I? My identity is found and defined in Christ. It's not about what I've done or can do. It is not about what I've accomplished; it's about what He's accomplished—in me, through me, around me, and (when necessary) *in spite of me.*

When I *don't* keep my eyes on the things that matter, when I fail to find my identity in Christ, I feel like I never quite measure up to the expectations of others. Like most women, I want to appear as though I have it all together, which means keeping my weaknesses a closely guarded secret. I feel tempted to compare myself to others, which leads me to judge them as well as myself. When I define my identity by *what I've done* rather than *who He is,* failure and hard times seem more overwhelming. It's harder to see the abundant life He's promised me. In short, I get lost when my eyes are turned towards my own roles, responsibilities, actions, wins, and losses. Those things are what I do. They aren't who I am. Who I really am is defined by who He is. The minute I lose sight of that, things go haywire.

CALLED BY NAME TO CLIMB

It's hard to believe sometimes, but I know God knew what He was doing when He made me. He made me to be unique; there's no one like me in the whole world. And guess what? There's no one just like you either. He knew what He was doing when He knit you together. Psalms says that He "created [your] inmost being" (Psalm 139:13). He knows all your quirks and skills and talents and struggles and weaknesses. He knows you inside and out, and He loves every part.

It's easy, even for Christians, to see God sitting high on His throne apart from the world. But that's not who He is. He's an active, ever-present, and caring Father. The Bible says, "He has identified us as His own by placing the Holy Spirit in our hearts" (2

IT'S HARD TO BELIEVE SOMETIMES, BUT I KNOW GOD KNEW WHAT HE WAS DOING WHEN HE MADE ME.

Corinthians 1:22a, NLT). When He looks at us, He sees us for who and what we really are: His children, the ones for whom He sent His Son and the ones on whom He poured out His Spirit. If you are in Christ, then that's who you are. He knows you by name—more intimately than you've ever been known.

Earlier, I mentioned how the mountains of Brazil have helped me learn and remember so much about God. There's no denying there is just something special about mountains. Their majesty and beauty can render us completely still and awestruck as we take them in. However, when we face mountains of challenge, loss, fear, or pain in our lives, we're often still and awestruck for another reason: fear. We are trying to figure out how we will get over, around, or past the mountain in front of us. Sometimes the mountain makes us feel alone, as if no one has ever faced what we're facing. We assume no one could understand or help. But the truth is, we all face mountains in our lives. You may be stuck on one right now, or maybe you just got over one. Or, maybe you're standing at the base of one and you're feeling more alone than you've ever felt.

If that's where you are right now, I have wonderful news for you: *You are not alone.* The One who made you also made mountains. He knows every part of you, and He knows every part of the climb ahead of you. And, although it may not feel like much of a blessing in the moment, He's called you by name to climb it. But don't worry. He's there to climb it with you.

BUT THE TRUTH IS, WE ALL FACE
MOUNTAINS IN OUR LIVES. YOU MAY
BE STUCK ON ONE RIGHT NOW, OR
MAYBE YOU JUST GOT OVER ONE.

CHAPTER 2

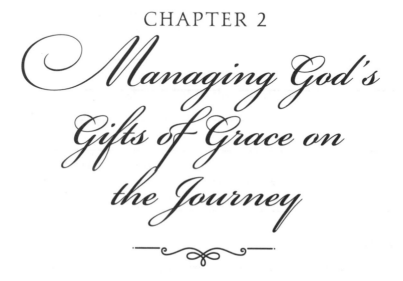

Managing God's Gifts of Grace on the Journey

*Each of you should use whatever gift you
have received to serve others, as faithful stewards
of God's grace in its various forms.*
—1 PETER 4:10

G od has poured out His rich blessings on me throughout my life. Now, when I say that, I tend to focus on the word *blessings*. Others, though, often try to focus on the word *rich*. It's true that my parents were extremely successful in business. Despite the humble home we lived in and the mostly *normal* lifestyle we maintained while I was growing up, Mom and Dad built a company that has now become a national phenomenon. Along with that success came financial wealth they never imagined. However, as we were growing up, I don't recall any time when my brothers and I saw ourselves as wealthy. Our parents were actually quite frugal; they said *no* a lot more often than they said *yes* when I asked them to buy me something. There were certainly no silver spoons in the Cathy

---

GOD HAS GIVEN US EVERYTHING
WE NEED FOR THE JOURNEY.

---

household! The way our parents lived (and taught us to live) modeled Psalm 24:1, "The earth is the LORD's and everything in it. The world and all its people belong to him" (NLT). As a result, we were raised to understand that God owns it all. We were just there to manage it.

When they passed away, my parents left my brothers and me not only the reins of Chick-fil-A, but also a financial inheritance. That inheritance, of course, came with an even bigger responsibility. Chick-fil-A has been a tremendous blessing to countless employees, investors, charities, and happy customers across the country for more than fifty years. As an heir to that legacy, it's one of my lifelong goals to be a faithful steward of everything my parents left me. Here's the thing, though: *legacy* and *money* are two different things. While money is important, it's not the *most* important resource in the world, and it certainly isn't the most significant gift my parents left me.

Mom and Dad understood that our heavenly Father has richly blessed all of us, pouring out His gifts of grace on His children regardless of where we are financially. God has given us everything we need for the journey. If we want to climb and conquer the mountains in our lives, we must be careful about how well we manage those blessings. That means being a good steward of everything God's put in our care—our relationships, our responsibilities, and (only then) our resources.

MANAGING RELATIONSHIPS

Sir John Templeton wrote, "Never forget: the secret of creating riches for oneself is to create them for others." Put another way, we are called to become pipelines of God's love, allowing the richness of His life and care to flow through us and into the lives of others. Those riches come in many forms. One of the most significant gifts we each receive is the community God's placed alongside us. Climbing up the mountain is always easier when there are people around to cheer us on! Quality relationships don't just happen though. They have to be cared for and cultivated with love. This is something my parents showed me every day. They always gave relationships—*other people*—a place of honor in their lives. Employees, neighbors, children, military service members, seniors, and everyone else were treated with respect, compassion, kindness, and care. We can learn so much and be so blessed by the people around us. The trick is to actually *tune our ears* to listen to and learn from them while we also *tune our hearts* to find ways to bless them back. We can do that by examining a few different key relationships.

FAMILY RELATIONSHIPS

At this point, it won't surprise you to hear that my parents were the most influential people in my life. They each lived out their values for everyone to see. Watching them go about their days, run a business, raise their children, serve in our church, and interact with people from all walks of life had a greater impact on me than I'll ever know. There are so many things I remember about my father: his work ethic, his continual care for those around him, but most of all, I recall his unwavering integrity. Dad always defined *integrity* as doing the right thing for the right reason, regardless of where you are or who you are with. He was always the same person, whether he was leading a high-level board meeting in the office, meeting a teenaged employee at a local Chick-fil-A, or reading a bedtime story to his children. Truett Cathy was always Truett Cathy.

Dad understood what it meant to be a channel of God's blessings to others, and he attributed his success more to simple servanthood than to business acumen. As Jesus taught, "Give, and it will be given to you. A good measure, pressed down, shaken together and running over, will be poured into your lap. For with the measure you use, it will be measured to you" (Luke 6:38).

While Dad was marked by his integrity and consistency, my mother, Jeannette, was the spiritual rock in our home. Her relationship with her heavenly Father was personal, vibrant, and radiant. She practically glowed with the love of God. That deep connection to God as Father was especially significant to her, because she grew up without knowing her earthly father. Her father abandoned his family when my mom was just a baby, so she never knew the love of a good dad like I did. For that reason, she clung to God. She absorbed every ounce of God's love, seeing it as a lifeline for the brokenhearted. She talked with God every day, every moment, always growing closer to Him. She held nothing back from her heavenly Father, and she clung to the promise of 1 Corinthians 13:12, "Now we see things imperfectly, like puzzling reflections in a mirror, but then we will see everything with perfect clarity. All that I know now is partial and incomplete, but then I will know everything completely, just as God now knows me completely" (NLT).

Mom's faith can be summed up in four words: "You can . . . *with God*." I can't remember ever hearing her complain about anything. No matter how scary the mountain or how steep the climb, she knew God had given her everything she needed to conquer it. And she didn't go through life with blinders on either. She wasn't afraid to look adversity in the face. Instead, she studied it. She looked for ways to find the treasure in the torment and bring out the positive in every trial. Whereas most people passively let hardships make them *bitter*, Mom used the pressure of adversity to make herself *better*.

That active spirit never slowed down; she was *always* in learning mode. She amassed a huge tool collection and learned how to fix pretty much everything in the house throughout her life. She taught herself oil painting at the age of sixty-five. She learned how to use a computer at eighty. She regularly memorized Scripture passages right up to her death at age ninety-two. Traveling, reading, talking with friends, working alongside some of the best leaders in the country—Mom saw every one of these things as opportunities to improve herself. Her example was a powerful inspiration to our family and our family business, and her legacy will continue for generations to come.

I know I talk about my parents a lot, but it's because they're a part of me. Their influence pours *out* of me because they spent a lifetime pouring it *into* me. They were intentional about leaving their children—and everyone else around them—a legacy that will outlast us all. Now, as John and I look at our four children, their spouses, and our grandchildren, we hope that we have made that same investment into our own family. So many people in the world see their parents and families as a curse, but my parents showed me how to be a blessing to my loved ones.

The most powerful legacy you can leave your children is your example. If you want to know what kind of men and women they'll grow up to be, I want to challenge you to take a good, hard look at what kind of man or woman you are right now. There's a good chance *that's* what your children will look like later. If you don't like what you see, then it's not too late to change it. Whatever your family situation has been, I pray that you can find a way to take the good, forgive the bad, and start building a new legacy for those who depend on you.

MENTOR RELATIONSHIPS

Parents have an incredible influence on their children's lives, but what happens if that influence is negative—or at least incomplete? Or, as is more often the case, what happens when God wants to *add to* the legacy He's providing through our parents? That's where godly mentors come in—and I was blessed with the best mentor in the world. Miss Johnnie Armstrong, who wrote the foreword for this book, has been a guiding force for almost my entire life. I first met Miss Johnnie when I was eight years old. My parents sent my brothers to Camp Ridgecrest and me to Camp Crestridge, a five-week overnight summer camp. The first person I met as we got out of the car and entered the dining hall was Miss Johnnie, the camp's assistant director. I could immediately tell there was something special about her; her joy and faith were infectious. I was just getting to know her that first summer, but even at that young age, I could tell she would become a tremendous influence in my life.

I cried when I had to leave camp (and Miss Johnnie) that first year, but I knew I'd see her again—and I did. I returned the next summer. And the next. And the next.   In all, I attended Camp Crestridge for eight summers as a camper and then served as part of the summer staff for another two years before college. Every moment talking to, working with, and learning from Miss

Johnnie was a gift. I *studied* her every chance I got, watching her
tireless dedication in serving the Lord with joy and enthusiasm.
I saw the sparkle in her eye that revealed how much she cared
about people whenever she talked with anyone, from her peers
to college-aged summer staff to eight-year-old first-timers. I
admired her wisdom and confidence when making critical decisions and leading others, especially after she became the director
of Camp Crestridge. I even came to appreciate the sternness on
her face and in her voice when she told me to "Straighten up!"
In some ways, even then, I could tell Miss Johnnie had high
expectations for me. I deeply respected her ability to challenge
others and expect nothing less than their very best. Her values
never wavered, regardless of the circumstances. She is and has
always been a woman of commitment and integrity, and she's
someone I strive to emulate to this day.

THE MOST POWERFUL LEGACY YOU CAN
LEAVE YOUR CHILDREN IS YOUR EXAMPLE.

My camp experiences under her leadership changed me in so
many ways. I learned how to engage in healthy relationships, make
wise decisions, walk in self-confidence, grow in my spiritual walk,
and have fun in my life in Christ. And so when I was asked to
serve as the Director for WinShape Camps for Girls in October,
2003, the first person I called was Miss Johnnie. Because my own
camp experiences as a child were so foundational to the woman
I'd become, I was honestly intimidated by the position. I couldn't
imagine trying to fill the same role as the woman I so greatly
admired. With her counsel, I took the position and tried my best to
be for those girls what Miss Johnnie was for me. For ten summers
of my life, she modeled what it meant to be a godly camp director,

to serve young girls, and to point them to Jesus through the camp experience. I owe so much of what I managed to accomplish in my own thirteen years as a camp director to what Miss Johnnie taught me. I am truly indebted to her.

Mentors have enormous potential in our lives. They add a richness and flavor to our experiences that we often can't find at home. They provide a much-needed outside perspective to challenges we may not see clearly. They serve as a guide to help us over the hills and mountains we're facing—often because they've *already* conquered those same obstacles themselves. I've had the opportunity to mentor many young girls and women throughout my life, and I always seem to learn as much from them as they do from me. Mentorship is a beautiful gift, and it's a powerful way to extend your legacy far beyond the boundaries of your own family. If you aren't actively seeking ways to invest into the lives of others, give it a try. There are people all around you who could benefit from your experience.

LOVING YOUR NEIGHBOR

Your legacy doesn't have to stop with your family and a handful of people you may mentor throughout your life. Rather, you have the chance to spread your legacy every day to everyone around you, friends and strangers alike. My father was a master at this. Even in business, he valued relationships more than anything. His employees became like family to him as he learned about their lives and dreams. He truly wanted each one to succeed, and he put his money where his heart was. He provided opportunities for education, bought clothes for them, and was always watching out for big and small ways to meet their needs. He loved to "work the floor" at neighborhood Chick-fil-A restaurants. He'd pop in and walk through the place sharing laughs and handshakes with team members and customers. He loved hearing their stories and brightening their day. And, in doing so, he was making an investment in their lives. He was showing them that they *mattered* and that he cared for them. It was so fun to watch him work a crowd!

IF YOU TRULY WANT TO MAKE A DIFFERENCE IN THIS WORLD, STRIVE TO CONNECT WITH PEOPLE THROUGH THE POWER OF RELATIONSHIP.

Often, the best gift we can give someone is simply our love, respect, and attention. The people around us need to feel valued; they need to know they're worthy of our time and effort. That can be as simple as a smile and a polite word to the cashier at the grocery store while you're checking out. Or, if it's someone you see regularly, it can be a consistent demonstration of your interest in their life. We're called to be vessels of God's love, and that love is most powerfully demonstrated in our relationships, our heart-to-heart interactions with other people. If you truly want to make a difference in this world, strive to connect with people through the power of relationship.

MANAGING RESPONSIBILITIES

In addition to the relationships God's showered upon us, He's also given us a set of core responsibilities to manage for His glory. On the surface, *responsibility* may sound more like an obligation or an edict than a gift of grace, but I want to challenge you to view it from God's perspective. Look beyond the "stuff" we so often get distracted by, things like wealth, status, power, popularity, and even the people in our lives. When I first looked deeply into my relationship with Christ through the lens of stewardship, He put three key truths on my heart:

1. I am His child.
2. I am His follower.
3. I am His light.

These truths may not be what you were expecting in a section called "Managing Responsibilities," but they revolutionized how I view my duty to God and stewardship of His blessings. Let's unpack them to get at the deeper meaning this insight has for every believer.

I AM HIS CHILD

First and foremost, I am a child of God. Sadly, that's a fact too many of us take for granted. Not so for my mother. She *delighted* in her heavenly Father. Because she never knew her earthly father, it was a life-altering realization for her to discover she could become a child of the King simply by choosing to accept God's gift of salvation through Christ. She accepted His love and presence into her life at only five years old, but she remembered that moment clearly throughout her life. As a young girl, I remember my mother's voice filling the house as she sang Harriet Buell's beautiful hymn, "I'm a Child of the King."

> *My Father is rich with houses and lands; He holdeth the wealth of the world in His hands. Of rubies and diamonds of silver and gold His coffers are full; He has riches untold. I'm a child of the King, a child of the King. With Jesus my Savior, I'm a child of the King.*

Mom often talked about her fatherless childhood, but she would always add, "But don't feel sorry for me! I have a perfect Father!" To paraphrase what she told me every time I left the house as a teenager, she knew *who* she was and she knew *whose* she was. She was a child of the King.

Unlike my mother, I was blessed with a wonderful earthly father. Having Truett Cathy for a dad was a tremendous blessing, but it also came with tremendous responsibilities. I knew that I represented him in everything I did. If I did something stupid as a teenager, nobody would say, "Did you hear about Trudy?" Instead, they'd say, "Did you hear what *Truett Cathy's daughter* did?" If I failed as a Chick-fil-A Operator, people would see it as my father's failure, not mine. If I acted like a spoiled, entitled brat my whole life, people would think Truett Cathy was a bad father. I love and respect my father too much to let *anyone* use me as an excuse for thinking poorly of him. Now, if I feel that way about my earthly father, how much more seriously do you think I take my responsibility to my heavenly Father? My mother's example made it impossible for me to deny my role as a child of God; I am indeed a daughter of the Most High. As such, I represent Him to everyone I meet—so I better represent Him well.

I AM HIS FOLLOWER

Second, I am a follower of Jesus Christ. As such, I'm committed to a lifetime of obedience to Him. That means I have a great responsibility to demonstrate and share my faith with others. I'd like to say that I've always been a natural at managing this responsibility, but that wouldn't be true. In fact, I've struggled greatly in this area throughout my life. God has brought about growth, of course, but that growth did not come easily.

For example, I mentioned in the previous chapter that I had some initial reluctance when John first expressed his call into international missions. "Initial reluctance" is putting it mildly. The truth is, I *hated* the idea. I was not receptive to this prospect in any way, and I shut John down time after time when he wanted to explore the possibility. I had gotten comfortable with my life. I was

content with my home, my car, and the *stuff* around me. I adored
my career as a full-time wife and mother to our (then) two children.
I loved living close to my entire family. In short, I had absolutely
zero interest in stripping everything in my life to the bone to serve
people in a different country! I was convinced John wasn't hearing
God clearly.

After weeks and months of this tension, I found myself
listening to music in my house as I went about my day. The song
"Let Me See This World Dear Lord" came on, and the words of the
song got firmly planted in my brain—and heart. The lyrics spoke
of seeing the world through the eyes of Christ and taking on His
heart toward others. Each word brought new waves of conviction.
Was I really more concerned with the conveniences of my comfortable life than I was about God's prompting to go meet the needs of
others? I'm not saying *everyone* should pack up and hit the foreign
mission field, but this was something God was calling my family
into. John heard it with crystal clarity; the only problem was my
resistance. Once I set my fears and selfishness aside, I realized that
I was hearing it too. The desire to be obedient to this call grew
stronger and stronger over the coming weeks. Not long afterward,
John and I were on a flight to Brazil with our children to start what
was probably the best decade of our lives!

I need to be honest though. God's still working on me in this
area of responsibility. I haven't gotten it all figured out yet, and I
still miss the mark at times. However, even when I don't *like* what
He's calling me to do, I can at least admit that my God is calling
me to follow Him *somewhere*. You can't call yourself a follower of
Christ if you aren't willing to actually *follow* Him. If you struggle
in this area like I do, I encourage you to set your comforts aside
for a while. Simplify your life, cut out the clutter, quiet the noise,
and then listen for the guiding voice of the One calling you. He
has plans for you, and He knows the mountains He's calling you to

climb. Trust Him enough to take that first step on what may be the most exciting, rewarding journey of your life.

I AM HIS LIGHT

Of all the responsibilities God's entrusted to me, I believe the greatest is the call to be His light in the world. After a lifetime of walking with the Lord, I still can't believe He trusts me so much as to send me out as His ambassador, as His light in a dark world. When we receive the salvation that God freely offers through Jesus's death and resurrection, we instantly become the temple of God; His Spirit dwells within us and, in a very real way, we are flooded with the light of His love. As the apostle Paul says in 2 Corinthians 4:7, "But we have this treasure in jars of clay to show that this all-surpassing power is from God and not from us." We are literally cracked clay pots filled with the most precious treasure in the universe!

In John 8:12, Jesus calls Himself the "light of the world." Then, in Matthew's Gospel, He uses that same language to describe those who follow Him. He commands, "You are the light of the world . . . let your light shine before others, that they may see your good deeds and glorify your Father in heaven" (Matthew 5:14–16). Wherever we go and whatever we do, the light of Christ should shine radiantly through our lives. We shine that light when we dedicate who we are and what we do to Him. We live out His call to be the light of the world when we follow the command of Ecclesiastes 9:10, "Whatever your hand finds to do, do it with all your might." So whether I'm playing the piano, teaching, singing, encouraging, mentoring, hosting guests in our home, supporting camp, leading a team, participating in a business meeting, comforting a friend, or rejoicing with another, I have determined to do it with all my might. My Father deserves nothing less.

I've been blessed to have had many wonderful examples of God's children shining His light. My mother carried the light of God with her; her very presence could bring joy and peace to a room. My father carried the light of God into the workplace; he cared for his customers and employees alike. Miss Johnnie carried the light of God as she ministered to countless girls over the years; she lives what she teaches and continues to impact innumerable lives, just as she impacted my own. It is my sincere prayer that I present myself to God each day as a vessel for His light. Only God's light can illuminate the world and enable people to see the Savior, and carrying that light is the greatest responsibility we can bear.

MANAGING RESOURCES

God not only gives us relationships and responsibilities to manage but also several resources. In Luke's Gospel, Jesus says, "From everyone who has been given much, much will be demanded; and from the one who has been entrusted with much, much more will be asked" (Luke 12:48). This may sound like an edict, but I believe Jesus's words are a statement of honor and trust. He pours His grace and mercy into our lives so that we can bless others. Or, put another way, *we are blessed to be a blessing*. As God promised Abraham, "I will make you a great nation, and I will bless you; I will make your name great, *and you will be a blessing*" (Genesis 12:2, emphasis added).

We see this throughout Scripture and in the lives of faithful stewards. The poor widow in Luke 21:1–4 didn't have much to give, but just look at the heart of worship she possessed! She may not have given much money, but she gave her whole heart—and that's the kind of attitude I think God's looking for. That's what Miss Johnnie has. She may not possess much by the world's definition of wealth and success, but she used what she *did* possess to change the lives of more people than most of us will ever impact. The same can be said of Mother Teresa and countless other missionaries who have given all they had in service to God and for the benefit of others.

God gives each of us different gifts, but at the heart of every one is the gift of God's grace. Remember, everything we have is His. Psalm 24:1 proclaims, "The earth is the LORD's, and *everything* in it, the world, and all who live in it" (emphasis added). Speaking to Job, God declares, "Who has a claim against me that I must pay? *Everything* under heaven belongs to me" (Job 41:11, emphasis added). Everything means . . . well, *everything.* It's not just about our money and possessions; it's about all that we have. As faithful stewards of God's grace, I believe there are four key resources we must manage for His glory: our money, time, talents, and influence. Let's take a quick look at each one.

MANAGING MONEY

I said at the start of this chapter that many people hear the name Cathy and immediately think about the wealth my parents built throughout their lives. The thing is, though, my parents themselves rarely focused on or worried about money. My brothers and I were raised with the understanding that God owns everything; our money was simply one tool He had entrusted us to manage. Mom and Dad taught us biblical principles for handling money—things my husband and I not only passed on to our children but also still do ourselves to this day. We tithe, giving God the first ten percent of everything we make. We save for the future and for big purchases, set and work toward financial goals, and spend wisely. Based on my parents' example, John and I have lived on a monthly budget from day one of our marriage. We taught our children to do the same. Even after all this time, living on a budget seems perfectly normal to us.

In the early years of our marriage, John and I were like most young couples. We worked hard, pinched pennies, and sometimes barely made ends meet. Running to Mom and Dad for money every other week wasn't an option; instead, we watched in awe as

God provided when things seemed hopeless. As we grew in our careers and as we saved long-term, things loosened up a bit. Whether we had a little or a lot at any given time, though, we always viewed our money as a gift of God's grace. He intends for us to enjoy it, but, more importantly, we are to be a channel of His blessing to others. God demands a generous heart through which He can pour His grace onto others.

TO TRULY HONOR GOD'S FINANCIAL
BLESSING IN OUR LIVES, WE MUST ALWAYS
BE ON THE LOOKOUT FOR OPPORTUNITIES
TO GIVE OVER AND ABOVE THE TITHE.

You may be reading this and thinking, *Well, that sounds nice, but I can't afford to give. I'm barely getting by as it is.* I get it. It's usually hard to feel rich when you're worried about paying the electric bill. However, I want to challenge you to change your perspective. Compared to most of the world, you *are* rich. In his book, *The Legacy Journey*, Dave Ramsey points out that Americans making just $34,000 are in the top one percent of income earners in the world.[1] If you have a car, more than one pair of shoes, a roof over your head, and clean water, you are living a life of luxury many people in the world could never even imagine. I always *knew* this, but living and working with the poor in Brazil brought this truth to life in an unforgettable way. As my son John says, "God wants to use us in His mission *outside* suburban America."

I believe giving starts with the tithe to your local church (Malachi 3:10), but it shouldn't end there. To truly honor God's financial blessing in our lives, we must always be on the lookout for

---

1   Dave Ramsey, *The Legacy Journey*, (Nashville: Ramsey Press, 2014), 20.

opportunities to give over and above the tithe. I'm not saying you need to give to every person who asks for money or every charity that sets up a tent at the front door of your grocery store. Being wise stewards means making sure the money you give is managed well and actually gets to the people you're trying to help. Do your due diligence with your giving, just as you would with your investing. And then, when you're sure you've identified some truly worthy causes, make financial giving a priority in your budget.

MANAGING TIME

While money is important, it's not the only gift we have to give. In fact, money is often not even the *hardest* gift to give. Many times, the biggest sacrifice we can make is giving our time to others in need. Time and money should be managed the same way. Both are finite resources, meaning you only have so much to work with. Both present a million different opportunities to waste what you've got. Both can make an enormous impact on the world around you. And poor management of either will leave you sick, tired, stressed, and miserable. Time is the great equalizer; God's given all of us— from kings to businessmen to pastors to homemakers—the same amount of time every day. You can't add one minute to your day, no matter how noble or wealthy you are. That means each of us is responsible for the wise management of what we've been given.

Of course, you may say that you have no time to give. That kind of sounds like the money argument, doesn't it? The truth is, we *all* have time to give; it's a simple matter of choices. It's time for some tough love here. If your day is packed wall to wall with no breathing room, it's because you've said *yes* to too many things. You and only you control where and how you spend your time. It's not up to your boss; you can find another job. It's not up to your children; you're the parent and you make the decisions. It's not up to the dozen nonprofits you may volunteer for; you can trim down your list of commitments. Everything you're doing today is taking up your time because you've allowed it to. My suggestion? Review your daily, weekly, and monthly commitments and cut out whatever isn't truly necessary. Time is too precious to waste, so make sure you're honoring God by using the gift of time to its fullest. That might mean saying *yes* to new opportunities, and it might mean saying *no* to some old ones. Only you get to choose, so do it with some intentionality.

MANAGING TALENT

Managing time effectively isn't only about *where* you spend your time; it's about *how* you spend your time. You want to leverage your talents, skills, and natural abilities in whatever you do. Serving on your church's financial team may sound like a worthy commitment,

GOD GIVES US HUNDREDS OF OPPORTUNITIES EVERY DAY TO IMPACT SOMEONE OR SOMETHING.

but if you hate math and don't know how to budget, you're wasting your time and theirs. You'll be completely miserable and ineffective in the position and, even worse, you're filling a spot that would be much better served by someone else. Here's a simple, basic rule of thumb: If you don't have the talent or passion for what's being asked of you, it's not a fit. God filled you with gifts and abilities that can and should be used for His glory. That only happens when we find out what we're good at and focus our time and efforts on those things.

MANAGING INFLUENCE

Influence is one of the most important, most powerful, and most overlooked commodities in the world. We too often take it for granted. We think some people have it and some don't. That's not true at all. Influence simply means having an impact on someone or something. It's not about having a big platform, leading a large company, or even having the ability to speak in front of a group. It's just about making an impact on someone—*anyone*. Regardless of who we are or what position we hold in life, each of us impacts every person and every situation we encounter. A simple smile can influence the day of a person in sorrow. Words of encouragement can bring faith and courage to someone who is struggling. Loving our families well can impact future generations. We all carry more influence than we realize, so don't tell me you aren't influential. God gives us hundreds of opportunities every day to impact someone or something. Once you recognize that fact, you can start to become more aware of when, where, and how you're using your influence for His glory.

HIS GIFTS FOR HIS GLORY

Maturing in our faith can sometimes feel like an impossible mountain to climb. There have been times in my life when I thought I was making great headway only to realize I was heading in the wrong direction! There have been other times when "life happened" despite my best efforts and the mountain I thought I was climbing turned out to be a cliff I fell off of. The life we are called to live, I believe, goes against our nature in many ways. Even the apostle Paul struggled with this. He wrote in the book of Romans:

I do not understand what I do. For what I want to do I do not do, but what I hate I do. . . . For I know that good itself does not dwell in me, that is, in my sinful nature. For I have the desire to do what is good, but I cannot carry it out. For I do not do the good I

want to do, but the evil I do not want to do—this I keep on doing.
(ROMANS 7:15, 18–19)

Paul touches on an issue that should be familiar to all of us. We may know what we should do in a given situation, but following through with it isn't always our first instinct. It cuts against what Paul calls our *sinful nature.* I call it *self-absorbed.*

Our human nature draws our attention inward, but, as children of God and His ambassadors in the world, we are called to live our lives openly, generously, humbly, and lovingly. Those things require us to take our eyes off ourselves and look at other people—and that is no easy task. It's as though there's a war raging within us between our selfish human nature and our call to be loving and selfless. How are we to settle the conflict? Paul gives us the perfect starting point as he continues his discussion above: "Thanks be to God, who delivers me through Jesus Christ our Lord" (Romans 7:25). God's given us everything we need for the journey. More than that, He's directing every step on the path. Paul writes in Galatians, "Those who belong to Christ Jesus have crucified the flesh with its passions and desires. Since we live by the Spirit, let us keep in step with the Spirit" (Galatians 5:24–25). I love that phrase, "keep in step with the Spirit." Because of God's grace, we can live beyond our self-absorbed human nature and live our lives—and climb our mountains—in step with Him.

Know–Be–Live

KNOW

Consider 1 Peter 4:10, "Each of you should use whatever gift you have received to serve others, as faithful stewards of God's grace in its various forms." What gifts of grace have you received?

_____

_____

_____

_____

_____

_____

_____

BE

Take an honest look at how you manage your relationships, responsibilities, resources, and any other gifts of grace God's entrusted to you. How well are you managing these resources for Him? In what ways are you succeeding and/or falling short?

_____

_____

_____

_____

_____

Know–Be–Live

LIVE

Reflect on Luke 12:48, "From everyone who has been given much, much will be demanded; and from the one who has been entrusted with much, much more will be asked." What are some practical steps you can take to use these gifts to further God's kingdom?

CHAPTER 3

Scaling toward Significance

By the grace of God I am what I am.
—1 CORINTHIANS 15:10 (NLT)

I n the first chapter of this book, we focused at length on our identity in Christ. We tackled *who* we are and, more importantly, *whose* we are. Now I want to move onto another important question: *What* are we doing here? How do we discover what God wants us to do during our time on earth? How do we know we're climbing the right mountains? You see, answering *who* reveals our identity, but understanding *what* reveals our purpose. And, no matter who, what, or where we are, our purpose is to glorify God. We just have to figure out the best way to do that with our unique circumstances, gifts, talents, and calling.

UNIQUELY DESIGNED FOR SIGNIFICANCE

We've seen that God knits us together piece by piece, intentionally crafting us into wonderfully unique individuals. We're like walking, talking snowflakes; no two people are just alike. If He went to such painstaking detail crafting me as precisely as He did, there must have been a reason, right? He must have had some plans in mind for me. I believe He gave me a passion for mentoring young girls because He wanted me to mentor young girls. I think He gave me a knack for public speaking because He wanted me to speak in public. I'm sure He gave me an entrepreneurial spirit because He wanted me to launch new ideas and initiatives into existence. He custom-built me to do everything He knew He'd call me to do. He's the designer; He knows more about me than I do! That's why He so often brings me opportunities I wasn't expecting. He knows the secret to the success of that opportunity is locked away somewhere inside me, and He's ready to bring it out and put it to use. He does the same with you. In this way, He's uniquely designed each and every one of us for significance.

HE UNIQUELY DESIGNED ME ...

Say that phrase out loud and personalize it: *He has uniquely designed me for significance.* Do you believe that? Do you believe He has big things in store for you, that He created you with a purpose in mind? I do. I don't know you, but I know God has big plans for you. That's why He made you who you are. He crafted your *who* (your identity) so you could accomplish your *what* (your purpose). Even the prophet Jeremiah struggled to accept this truth, but God reminded him, "Before I shaped you in the womb, I knew all about you. Before you saw the light of day, I had holy plans for you: A spokesman to the nations— that's what I had in mind for you" (Jeremiah 1:5, MSG). God may not be calling you to be a "spokesman to the nations," but He did design you this way for a reason.

We each have a God-given plan and purpose that no one else can fulfill, and God's given us what we need to get the job done. That's why it's so silly to waste our time fretting about what gifts *other people* have. God gifted them for *their* task; those same gifts may not make a lick of difference to the job God's called you to do. That's like being envious of your neighbor's house key. Sure, you could get a key just like it, but it wouldn't open *your* front door! *That* key was designed to fit *that* lock. If you remove the gift from its purpose, you lose its usefulness. God is the ultimate artist; He crafted every piece in detail and on purpose. And, as Paul argues in Romans 9:20, "Who do you think you are to question God? Does the clay have the right to ask the potter why he shaped it the way he did?" (CEV). Of course not. In the same way, we shouldn't look up to the heavens and ask God why He didn't bless us in the exact same way He blessed someone else. He didn't equip you to fulfill another person's purpose. He equipped you to fulfill your own.

. . . FOR SIGNIFICANCE

I think one of the biggest challenges we face in our walk with God is valuing godly significance more than worldly success. We get so distracted by what we think success looks like—impressive careers, nice cars, big houses, and so on. But I believe *real* success is gaining significance by living out the purpose we were each designed for. The world seems to define success by what we're able to *take* from life. Godly significance, however, is more concerned with how much I *give* my life. Significance happens when your life adds value, when you give out of what you've been given. We're blessed to be a blessing, remember? As the apostle Paul explains, "I have been a constant example of how you can help those in need by working hard. You should remember the words of the Lord Jesus: 'It is more blessed to give than to receive' " (Acts 20:35, NLT). In the search for significance, it's not about how long I live; it's about how much I give.

That means giving our *whole* selves, by the way. Too often, we try to compartmentalize our lives. We effectively tell God He can have *this* but not *that*. We want Him to *bless* our whole lives, but we don't want to *offer* Him our whole lives. True significance in our walk with Christ means putting that unhealthy separation to rest. I like to look at it according to the S.H.A.P.E. model developed by Erik Rees.[2] He teaches that there are five key things that shape a person for ultimate fulfillment:

1. **S**piritual gifts (God-given abilities)
2. **H**eart (what we love to do; passion)
3. **A**bilities (natural inclinations; talents)
4. **P**ersonality (disposition and temperament)
5. **E**xperiences (life circumstances; family, education, vocation, etc.)

2 Erik Rees, *S.H.A.P.E.: Finding and Fulfilling Your Unique Purpose for Life*, (Grand Rapids: Zondervan, 2006).

Using this model, Pastor Rick Warren explains, "Your ministry will be most effective and fulfilling when you are using your gifts and abilities in the area of your heart's desire in a way that best expresses your personality and experience."[3] That means your version of significance will look much different than someone else's. God made each of us to accomplish His specific purpose in our own lives; you can't win the race by crossing someone else's finish line.

LIVING OUT GOD'S PLAN EVERY DAY

We live lives of significance when we live out God's calling for us, but that begs the question: How do we discover what it is God wants us to do? It would be easier if we were born with individualized instruction manuals detailing what we should do, where we should go, and who we should work with throughout our lives. Sadly, it's not that simple. Over the years, as I have attempted to live out God's plan for my life, I have come up with three questions that have kept me on track. These questions help keep me attuned to God's purposes in my life:

1. Am I willing to listen to God?
2. Am I willing to keep an open mind with God?
3. Am I willing to follow through on what I hear from God?

Let's dig into these three questions and see how they can lead us in living a life of significance that honors the Lord.

AM I WILLING TO LISTEN TO GOD?

Hearing God's voice seems like an alien concept to many people. This point was made painfully clear to me as I was working on

---

3 Rick Warren, "Never Forget How God SHAPED You for Ministry," *Pastors.com*, April 17, 2015, https://pastors.com/never-forget-how-god-shaped-you-for-ministry/.

this book. A well-known daytime talk show host suggested the vice president of the United States had a mental illness because he dared to believe that God speaks to him in prayer. She was stunned that this man, a devout Christian, had the audacity to believe the Bible. She couldn't understand the concept of prayer as a two-way conversation, so she used it as an opportunity to insult the vice president. I'd like to say I'm surprised . . . but I'm not. Many people simply can't wrap their brains around the fact that our God is an active, living Lord who still talks to His children today. Jesus tells us, "My sheep listen to my voice; I know them, and they follow me" (John 10:27). What we know as faith others will see as insanity. That's okay. We're living *our* lives, not theirs.

Revelation 3:20 tells us what will happen if we truly hear the voice of our Lord. Jesus says, "Here I am! I stand at the door and knock. If anyone hears my voice and opens the door, I will come in and eat with that person, and they with me." Here's what I want you to see in this verse: *God is speaking to us.* He is trying to get our attention. He calls out and says, "Here I am!" Yet how many of us truly focus our ears and hearts on what God is saying? How many times does His call go unanswered? I've been honest about the fact that I'm still working on this area of my faith. When God called John and me into missions, I stuck my fingers in my ears and ignored Him for as long as I could. I stubbornly closed myself off to what He was saying for two-and-a-half years until He finally got my attention in an undeniable way. Now, looking back, I picture Jesus standing at the door of my heart and knocking, just as He describes in Revelation. He was calling, "Here I am!" but I didn't listen. I wasted so much time ignoring what He so desperately wanted to tell me.

When we actually listen to Him, God will direct us toward the plan He has had for us for all eternity. This was His promise to the prophet Isaiah. He declared, "I am the LORD your God, who teaches you what is best for you, who directs you in the way you should go" (Isaiah 48:17). Before He can teach us or direct us, though, we must be willing—and able—to listen. That means learning how to hear His voice. I want to suggest three ways we can learn to get better at hearing Him when He speaks.

First, we have God's Word. If you want to hear God's voice, start by reading His Word. Writing to his young apprentice, Timothy, the apostle Paul notes, "All Scripture is God-breathed and is useful for teaching, rebuking, correcting and training in righteousness, so that the servant of God may be thoroughly equipped for every good work" (2 Timothy 3:16–17). We would all live much happier, more fulfilled and significant lives if we simply read the Bible.

HAVE YOU EVER HESITATED TO ASK GOD TO SHOW YOU SOMETHING BECAUSE YOU WERE ACTUALLY AFRAID OF THE ANSWER?

Second, we know God's character. God will never ask us to do anything that is against His moral will. He is unchanging; His perfect integrity doesn't change day to day. The book of Hebrews notes, "Jesus Christ is the same yesterday and today and forever" (Hebrews 13:8). The apostle James wrote, "Every good and perfect gift is from above, coming down from the Father of heavenly lights, who does not change like shifting shadows" (James 1:17). What does that mean to us? Whenever we think we hear God calling us to do something, we can test that call against what we know about God. If it's something that is clearly outside His character or contrary to what we know in His Word, we can be sure it's not God who's speaking to us in that moment. We can filter that message out because we know it's inconsistent with who God is.

Third, we can listen for God's voice. This one may seem uncomfortable if you, like the TV host I mentioned earlier, don't believe God still speaks in an active and living way. However, look at the promise God made to the prophet Isaiah, "Whether you turn to the right or to the left, your ears will hear a voice behind you saying, 'This is the way; walk in it' " (Isaiah 30:21). He assured the prophet that, when he needed direction, he would hear God's voice. That promise holds true for us today. Although we may never hear His audible voice with our ears, we can still hear Him with our hearts. God is Almighty; He doesn't need our ears to get His message across. He will make Himself and His message known deep within us—in the core of our beings—if we are diligently seeking Him. He promises in Jeremiah 29:13, "You will seek me and find me when you seek me with all your heart." Even when we can't hear Him or when we've shut ourselves off from His call, He will communicate through pastors, friends, opportunities, experiences, and anything else. When I had shut myself off to His call to missions, He ultimately reached me by surprise through a song on the radio. You never know how, when, and where He will get through to you. We can just be sure that He will.

AM I WILLING TO KEEP AN OPEN MIND WITH GOD?

Have you ever hesitated to ask God to show you something because you were actually afraid of the answer? I have. Sometimes we get in a spiritual rut and start to view God as Santa Claus instead of the almighty, all-knowing Creator of the universe. You see, Santa brings us presents. He only brings things we want, things that bring *fun* into our lives. God's not like that. He only wants what's best for us, of course, but He knows that what's *best* isn't always what's the most *fun*. The truth we need to hear from Him is often hard to swallow; we don't like what He has to say and we don't want to do what He tells us to do. People don't usually run away from Santa Claus, but they run away from God all the time.

We just read the passage in Jeremiah 29:13, "You will seek me and find me when you seek me with all your heart." That's a promise. The Hebrew word translated as *seek* literally means to look diligently or search intently until you find what you're looking for. If we eagerly and sincerely seek to hear from God, we will. We have His assurance, " 'I will be found by you,' declares the LORD" (Jeremiah 29:14). There are times, however, when we don't want to find Him. We don't want to hear from Him. We know what He's going to say, and so we avoid Him. We'd rather carry on with what *we* want to do ourselves than change our plans, attitudes, commitments, and behaviors to carry out His will for our lives. And so we shut ourselves off, going through the motions of our faith while we have our fingers stuck in our ears and a blindfold over our eyes.

YOU'RE EITHER AT THE FOOT OF A MOUNTAIN LOOKING UP, ON THE BACK SIDE OF A MOUNTAIN WORKING YOUR WAY DOWN, OR SOMEWHERE IN THE MIDDLE.

This close-mindedness toward God is often the result of going through some hardship or tragedy. Maybe you've been through a difficult loss, such as a death or a broken relationship, and you're simply mad at God. Believe me, I've been there. Later in this book, I'll share some of the personal losses and hardships that have impacted my life. For now, just trust that I know the pain that can lead you to question whether or not God *really* cares. Fortunately, I was blessed with a wonderful mother who was open about her own struggles. She had a difficult childhood. I've already shared that she never knew her father. Her mother raised her as best she could, but her early years were a struggle. The family never had much. She wore old, tattered, hand-me-down clothes. She watched her mother struggle to pay the bills month after month. She never had what other families took for granted. Those struggles early in life often leave a person feeling mad, entitled, and bitter as they enter adulthood. Not so with my mother. She rose above the struggle and rejoiced in the blessings she *did* have. She refused to let bitterness rob her of her intimate relationship with the Lord.

I've walked with others who handled their pain differently. I've seen as friends held tightly to hurtful memories and difficult circumstances. The result was a life filled with anger and resentment. They allowed their wounds to make them bitter, not better. Bitterness is borne of pride; bitterness considers hard times and difficult circumstances to be unfair and unwarranted. It leads people to adopt a victim mentality and the sense that the whole world—and God—are out to get them. In a very real way, bitterness toward God causes people to raise their fists in the air and cry out to God, "How dare you do this to me!"

The hard truth is that none of us will make it through this life untouched by hardship and faith-shaking difficulties. Jesus Himself said, "In this world you *will* have trouble" (John 16:33, emphasis added). The prophet Isaiah wrote, "*When* the enemy comes in like a flood . . ." (Isaiah 59:19, NKJV, emphasis added). Scripture is clear here: Adversity will strike every one of us; it's unavoidable. What we can control, though, is our response to those troubles. Let's go back to these two passages to get the *complete* picture. In John 16:33, Jesus continues His thought, "In this world you will have trouble. But take heart! I have overcome the world." Similarly, God says through Isaiah, "When the enemy comes in like a flood, the Spirit of the LORD will lift up a standard against him" (Isaiah 59:19, NKJV). Yes, trouble is coming. You're either at the foot of a mountain looking up, on the back side of a mountain working your way down, or somewhere in the middle. That's life. But God has promised to not only be there in the midst of our suffering but also to see us safely through to the other side—if we let Him.

As God's children, we must learn to run *to* Him—not *away from* Him—in the face of difficulty. He is not some distant deity looking down on us from on high and only marginally concerned with our suffering. He is in it with us! He is involved in every step, invested in every decision. When we hurt, He hurts. When we cry, He cries. Not a single tear goes unnoticed by God; in fact, He *collects* our tears! David wrote in Psalm 56:8, "You keep track of all my sorrows. You have collected all my tears in your bottle. You have recorded each one in your book" (NLT). Our tears speak to God. They are precious to Him because *we* are precious to Him. Pride and bitterness keep our eyes fixed on the trouble, but humility lifts our gaze to the Father whose arms are open wide and ready to comfort us.

Now let's get back to the matter at hand. If we hold tightly to God and open our minds to whatever He wants to communicate, will He lead us into places we'd rather not go? Yes. Absolutely. He will lead us into things that are so far beyond us that we can't even conceive of them. He'll take us into terrifying situations in which all we can do is hold on even tighter to His hand and trust that He'll stay with us till the end. Look at Gideon. Look at David. Look at Paul. Look at Peter. Then look in the mirror. God has a plan for every circumstance of your life. He will walk you through them and then enable you to use that experience to further His kingdom. Staying on the path, though, requires us to keep an open mind to where He leads.

AM I WILLING TO FOLLOW THROUGH ON WHAT I HEAR FROM GOD?

Once we've learned how to listen to God and we've opened our minds to His direction, there's only one thing left to do: obey. This is where so many of us get stuck. But if you want to live a life of significance, you must be willing to go wherever God may lead. If He calls you to be a missionary, go. If He requires you to learn another language, learn it. If He calls you to take on a position you feel entirely unprepared for, step up. Don't use your fear as an excuse. If He calls you to do something, He will give you the ability to get the job done. As the author of Hebrews prays, "May the God of peace . . . equip you with everything good for doing his will, and may he work in us what is pleasing to him, through Jesus Christ, to whom be glory for ever and ever" (Hebrews 13:20–21).

Even when we commit ourselves to obey God's call, we may still feel inclined to play it safe by sticking to what we know best. I encourage you to resist that temptation. As Henry and Melvin Blackaby explain in their book, *What's So Spiritual About Your Gifts?*:

> God wants to use your life in a whole new world of opportunity beyond your areas of competence and experience. So never put limits on how God can use your life. Obey God and trust that He knows what He's doing in your life. Don't look at your abilities and natural talents alone and serve only in the areas you feel competent. If you do, you'll eliminate yourself from significant arenas of service. Learn to seek God's will and obey Him no matter how difficult and uncomfortable the assignment and no matter how high the cost—knowing we're called to accomplish those tasks not according to our own capacity, but according to the fully enabling power of the Holy Spirit.[4]

That's easier said than done, but it is absolutely vital for a productive, adventurous life with Jesus Christ. God hasn't prepared a mundane life for you; He's prepared a rich, abundant life of opportunity and adventure! If you've heard His voice and you know what He's calling you to do, don't let fear, doubt, or bitterness get in your way. You'll only rob yourself of blessings you can't even imagine.

---

4 Henry T. Blackaby and Melvin D. Blackaby, *What's So Spiritual About Your Gifts?* (Vereeniging: Christian Art, 2005), 30.

SIGNIFICANCE, NOT SUCCESS

I didn't always strive to climb toward significance rather than success. Even though I had great parents who consistently pointed me to Christ, I still got distracted by *success* at times. Other times, I knew very clearly what God wanted me to do on my journey toward significance, but I flatly refused. Or I misheard Him. Or I ignored Him. Despite the wins and losses, though, I always try to keep moving. I think pressing on, even when the way is dark, is one of the keys to living a significant life. Step by grueling step, I have learned as I've walked—a kind of on-the-job training in God's kingdom ways.

WE HAVE A LIMITED NUMBER OF DAYS ON EARTH TO ADD VALUE TO THIS LIFE.

That momentum is important. The Bible doesn't promise that we'll know the path *before* we embark on the climb; it tells us that God directs our steps *as we walk* with Him (Psalm 16:11; 25:4–5; 32:8). This reminds me of a scientific principle of kinetic energy that says a stationary object cannot change course. Well, of course it can't! If something is sitting still, how can it change direction? That seems obvious, but let's apply it to our spiritual lives. How often do we get stuck in one place waiting on God to show us every part of His plan? I know I've been there. There have been times when I've been too scared or confused (or selfish) to move a single step in any direction. But if I'm not moving, how can God direct my steps? I have to be willing to make a few missteps and trust that God will be there to redirect me in the way He's called me to go.

When God called me to international work, I had to prepare for and embark upon that mission. When I got married, I had no idea how to be a wife. When my first child was born, motherhood was entirely outside my experience. When God led me to direct a camp for girls, I wasn't sure I had what it took to get the job done. In each of these situations, I could have shut down, said no, or hidden from God. If I'm being honest, that's exactly what I've done a time or two. But that's not how I'm going to live a life of significance. To climb the mountain, I've got to take some steps. Those first steps are usually the hardest, but they're the ones that give you momentum that carries you the entire journey.

This kind of life can seem terrifying. It can also seem too big to grasp. So, let's close with a simple formula for living out your God-given purpose. I try to focus on three simple statements: obey God's leadership, nurture family relationships, and promote godly character in the next generation. I've put these together into a meditation that I repeat often and I'd like to share that with you here:

> Live life with open hands (give generously)
> And a grateful heart (express gratitude)
> As I climb (strive for excellence)
> With care (respect for others)
> And confidence (trust God)
> Each and every day.

This statement keeps me focused on living a life of significance. When I'm struggling, I turn it into a prayer. On days when a particular line of this meditation feels hard to say honestly, I search my heart for whatever's getting in the way of my goal to live wholly according to God's rich calling. We have a limited number of days on earth to add value to this life. Doing so takes intentionality and dedication, following closely behind our Lord. As we make one right step, and then another, and then another, we will climb mountains—one step at a time.

Know—Be—Live

KNOW

How have you defined success throughout your life? List goals or accomplishments that have made you feel successful or would make you feel successful in the future. Then make a similar list of things that would make or have made you feel as though your life has had genuine significance. Note any differences in your lists.

_____

_____

_____

_____

_____

_____

BE

What have you done in pursuit of that ideal of success or significance? What impact have those goals had on your personality, relationships, and walk with Christ?

_____

_____

_____

_____

_____

_____

_____

Know–Be–Live

LIVE

What steps can you take that will enable you to more fully live out the different aspects of the motivational statement we looked at earlier?

Live life with open hands (give generously)

_____

_____

And a grateful heart (express gratitude)

_____

_____

As you climb (strive for excellence)

_____

_____

With care (respect others)

_____

_____

And confidence (trust God)

_____

_____

Each and every day.

_____

_____

CHAPTER 4

Building a Firm Foundation

———◦❧◦———

Train up a child in the way he should go,
and when he is old he will not depart from it.
—Proverbs 22:6 (NKJV)

Parents have a surprisingly short amount of time to make a deep investment into their children. Eighteen years seems like an eternity when you're a child, but when you're a parent, you realize how quickly the years fly by. When John and I were first starting our family, older friends would say things like, "It goes by so fast." So many people used that line that John and I made a joke of it. Now, several decades later, we realize the joke was on us; those years really did fly by. As the old saying goes, "The days go slow, but the years go fast." When I watched my children walk across the stage at their high school graduations, I yearned for the days when they could barely crawl across the kitchen floor. As they left for college and then got married, John and I sat back and prayed that we had done all we could to give them a strong foundation for life.

Even with my children grown and gone, though, I know my days as a parent aren't over. The time of raising children is brief, but parenting continues for life. And, more importantly, the training and equipping we did for them has carried over into their marriages and into how they're raising their own children. Each generation has enormous potential to shape and mold the next several generations. What my parents instilled in me, I tried to instill into my children. Now, they are instilling it into *their* children. Four different generations are present in that one little snapshot, each one impacting and influencing the next. Parenting is truly one of our greatest responsibilities, so let's take a few moments to learn how to make the most of the time we have with our children.

A WORD ABOUT FAMILIES

Before we begin, let me take a second to address something you may be thinking. I know there are many, many different kinds of family situations. It may seem controversial these days, but I believe the *ideal* family situation is the biblical model of one father and one mother who are married and living in the home together. I was blessed to grow up in such a home. Others, however, are not. My own mother, for example, was raised in a single-parent home by a godly mother who worked tirelessly to take care of her child. I have enormous respect for hardworking parents in that situation who are doing everything they can to raise happy, healthy sons and daughters. Families break up for many different reasons, and those reasons are often outside our control. As I discuss raising children in this chapter, please know that these principles apply to married parents and single parents alike. Also, if you're reading this and you do not have children, I want to encourage you to keep reading. Aunts, uncles, family friends, teachers, and mentors have all poured into my life. Whether you don't have children *yet* or you *never* plan to, you can still make an enormous investment into the next generation, leaving a legacy of influence that will far outlast you.

GROWING STRONG ROOTS

If you want your children to fly as adults, you need to start by grounding them as children. No, I'm not talking about *grounding* as a punishment—although my children were no strangers to that. I'm talking about giving your children a strong foundation, a root system that will sustain and support them as they grow. Plants, for example, require fertile soil, sunlight, and plenty of water. When all three things are present, the roots are able to dig down deep and provide a foundation for life that continually supplies nutrients needed for growth and development. In the same way, we must provide our children with the nutrients they need to flourish. As John and I have traveled through this parenting journey, we have learned that raising healthy, happy, productive children who are ready to soar into adulthood requires three key ingredients: commitment, consistency, and kindness. When all three are present, your children will develop a strong foundation from which they can launch into the world.

BE COMMITTED

Commitment is an absolutely vital component of faith and family, but it is becoming hard to see in today's culture. We have become a society ruled by impulse and instant gratification. Many people seem to be unable to focus on one thing for more than five seconds before they get distracted and move on to the next shiny object. But that kind of fly-by-night, in-the-moment lack of attention and commitment cause faith to flounder and families to fall apart.

Lack of commitment causes us to become what the Bible describes as "double-minded" and "unstable in all [we] do" (James 1:8). We can see examples of this everywhere we look these days. A double-minded person says one thing and does another. A double-minded person starts off in one direction but then changes course at the first bump in the road. A double-minded person is constantly wavering, undecided, and inconsistent. This is not the kind of parents our children need. If we want to raise children who are grounded in the Lord and prepared to fly when they leave home, we must demonstrate commitment. We have to show them how to fight through the struggle when things get hard and model a commitment to long-term goals over short-term pleasure. We have to practice responsibility, duty, allegiance, and devotion. We have to do what we say we're going to do.

As John and I have walked this road in our faith, marriage, and parenting, we've identified four specific commitments every parent should model for their children:

1. Commitment to God.
2. Commitment to prayer.
3. Commitment to marriage.
4. Commitment to parenting.

The list can and should be much longer than these four, of course, but I think these are the big ones. If you can model these four commitments for your children, you'll get them off to a great start.

COMMITMENT TO GOD

The most important commitment we can model for our children is a deep and abiding commitment to God. You will never know how much your own faith walk will influence that of your children. They are always watching; if you take God seriously, there's a good chance they will too. That means making time for the Lord regularly, making worship and ministry a priority, and talking freely about your faith at home—especially around your children. It also means being careful about how you express your own fears and anxieties. If you tell your children that God will take care of all their needs, but then they see you anxiously pulling your hair out every time you sit down to pay the bills, what message do you think you're *really* communicating?

Psalm 37:5 says, "Commit your way to the LORD." Proverbs 4:25–27 says, "Let your eyes look straight ahead; fix your gaze directly before you. Give careful thought to the paths for your feet and be steadfast in all your ways. Do not turn to the right or the left; keep your foot from evil." Our eyes should be fixed on Him, following in His footsteps instead of looking around at all the worldly distractions that are shouting for our attention.

COMMITMENT TO PRAYER

As believers, our first and foremost relationship should be with our Savior. It should be obvious to all of us that no relationship can flourish without regular, deep conversation. That's all prayer is: our conversations with God. It's simply being transparent with Him and listening intently for His response. Prayer is something that John and I have always taken very seriously, both individually and in our marriage. We also have spent countless hours praying together for our children, speaking to God about each one, lifting them up by name, and praying over their specific needs. I can't imagine raising our four children without that regular time of prayer. That's where we've received the specific guidance and direction we've needed time and time again. I think raising children without prayer is like trying to drive cross-country without a GPS; you wouldn't know where you're going or what's coming next, and you wouldn't know how to navigate the twists and turns along the way.

Pray for your children and be specific in your prayers. Pray for them by name. Pray for each need, each opportunity, each trial and stress. Pray for their salvation. Pray for God's wisdom as they make education and career decisions. Pray for their future spouse and children. Pray for God's blessings to rain down upon them. Pray for their wisdom and responsibility in managing those blessings. Pray for the impact they can have on the world and in their community. Pray, pray, pray!

COMMITMENT TO MARRIAGE

According to Pew Research Center, "Fewer than half (46%) of U.S. children younger than eighteen years of age are living in a home with two married heterosexual parents in their first marriage."[5] That means more than half of our nation's children have either seen their parents go through a divorce or never attempt marriage. Given this reality, strong marriage relationships are obviously rare. Rarer still are strong, Christian marriages—lifelong partnerships in which God has formed one from two (Genesis 2:23–24).

---

5 Gretchen Livingston, "Fewer than half of U.S. children today live in a 'traditional' family," Pew Research Center, December 22, 2014, http://www.pewresearch.org/fact-tank/2014/12/22/less-than-half-of-u-s-children-today-live-in-a-traditional-family/.

A couple's love serves as the most powerful example a child has of the beauty of marriage and of a godly partnership. Those lessons carry over into his or her future relationships. If a son sees his parents laugh and play together, that's what he'll expect in his own marriage. If a daughter sees her father verbally abuse her mother (or worse), that's what she'll expect from her own husband. We teach our children from our example what a "normal" marriage is, so we must be careful to set the best example possible.

John and I are not perfect people, and we certainly have not had the perfect marriage. We've had arguments, disagreements, and a few rough spots. In fact, even before we were married, there was a time when I threw my engagement ring at him in a rage and threatened to call off the wedding! Thinking back on that after all these years makes me want to laugh *and* cry. Getting married at a young age compounded the pressure, and having children added to the friction. I love my husband more than anything in the world, but, boy, have we had some doozies! Here's what's important, though: Through it all, we never questioned our commitment to each other. We never allowed ourselves to consider, let alone threaten, a divorce. It simply wasn't an option. That commitment—both to each other and to God who had formed this union—has kept us laughing and loving for more than forty years now. Even today, we are still working on our marriage; there will never be a time this side of heaven when we get it *perfect*. However, we have never stopped trying. And we believe one of the greatest gifts we've given our children is the love we give to each other in our marriage.

COMMITMENT TO PARENTING

I have worn many hats throughout my life. I've been a wife, a business owner, an entrepreneur, a missionary, and so on. Of all the challenging roles I've had, though, none have come close to the challenges of my role as a mother. It is a breathtaking reality that God puts a brand-new life in the care of flawed human parents. There's no question about it: parents make mistakes. Every parent causes problems, even while trying to solve others. We all mess up a million times or more, but God is there to bring beauty from the ashes of our all-too-human mistakes. When you accept the role of parent, you truly begin one of life's greatest adventures. The highs will be higher and the lows will be lower than you ever imagined.

Those highs and lows are especially apparent during the teen years. It was that season, especially, when John and I had to remind our children that we were their *parents*, not their *friends*. We have always had (and still have) great relationships with all our children, but we had to make some decisions during those teen years that were, shall we say, *unpopular*. If you have teenagers (or if you were ever one yourself), you know what I'm talking about. As much as possible, though, John and I tried to be proactive in our approach. Our goal was to prepare our children beforehand for the challenges they'd face and to give them the tools and information they'd need to tackle those issues before they came up. One way we did that was with an "I Promise" contract for each child. This was an agreement we developed with the children that addressed the temptations we knew they'd deal with someday. The document also asked for the child's commitment to abstain from certain activities and to avoid certain temptations whenever possible.

Did this contract completely eliminate all trials, temptations, and teen drama? No, not even close. However, it did give us the opportunity to have hard discussions with our children, and it called on them to make their own commitments in some key areas. Engaging them at that level and putting some of the responsibility on their shoulders to honor their commitment was a crucial step in their development, maturity, and the trust that grew between parent and child.

MY PROMISE RING
PRESENTED TO JOY KATHRYN WHITE
MARCH 1995 FOR HER 15TH BIRTHDAY

With this ring, I promise, before God, my parents, my sister, and my brothers, that my body will remain pure and holy. I agree to restrain from any sexual conduct that would contradict Christian principles taught to me by my parents based on God's Holy Word. This ring will be a constant reminder to me of God's great love and faithfulness to live His life through me. Whenever tempted to give in to my sexual desires, this ring will help me recall Psalm 46:1: "God is my refuge and strength, a very present help in trouble."

Upon receiving this ring, I also promise to abstain from any use of alcohol, drugs, or tobacco. With this commitment, I can present to my future husband a vessel clean and beautiful. In turn, I ask the Lord to give to me a husband whose past has been equally committed to my Lord—never having yielded to premarital sex, alcohol, drugs, or tobacco. I am committed to search and wait for such a man, so that our lives together can begin within God's plan for marriage.

_____

Joy Kathryn White

Family Witnesses: _____

_____

_____

_____

_____

BE CONSISTENT

Commitments are critical for parents, but they're only effective if your children see you living out those commitments every day in every situation. That kind of consistency is a key part of your personal integrity. In a previous chapter, I discussed my father's integrity and defined it as doing the right thing for the right reason, regardless of where you are or who is with you. To that, I'd add that integrity includes honesty, transparency, trustworthiness, and consistency. That means being the same person all the time. There should be no disconnect between who you are and how you act when you're happy, sad, mad, or stressed. Your children need to know how you're going to react in almost any situation. That's not something you can simply *tell* them; that's something they learn by *watching* you. And trust me, they are *always* watching you.

Both of my parents modeled consistent lives of integrity. The values and beliefs they talked about were reflected in how they lived. They didn't just teach us the importance of faith; they showed us by taking us to church every Sunday. They didn't just teach us about giving; they showed us by tithing and by donating generously to important causes. They didn't just teach us to read our Bible; they showed us how by reading the Word every day. They didn't just tell us to show kindness and respect to other people; they showed us by doing the same to everyone they met. This isn't rocket science, you know. The bottom line is that your children will likely do whatever you do. So if you don't want them to cuss, smoke, drink, and lie, then you shouldn't cuss, smoke, drink, or lie yourself. If they see you doing something you've told them not to, they'll immediately see the disconnect and trust what you're *doing* more than what you're *saying*.

Also, as a matter of consistency, let me give you this warning. Your children know how to push your buttons. They know how to play mind games and how to play one parent off another. You cannot let them. John and I committed early on to stay steady and on the same page even in the most trying times. When our children fell into an emotional fit, we didn't go there with them. We let them kick and scream and whine while we stood our ground. Eventually, they learned that we weren't going to play their games. We taught them self-control by *demonstrating* self-control in the middle of their meltdowns.

While I'd like to say we got it right every time, I can't. We made plenty of mistakes, but those mistakes gave us even more opportunities to show our children what a life of consistency and integrity looks like. Instead of ignoring our failings or, even worse, denying them, we admitted our mistakes to our children. We weren't ashamed to come to them with a cooler head and ask for their forgiveness. After all, our children know when we mess up; the least we can do is admit it and give them a chance to demonstrate grace. If you never own up to your shortcomings with your children, you will subtly tell them they can't trust you. You'll also teach them by example that they don't need to admit their mistakes either. That's not the kind of man or woman you want to send off into the world.

BE KIND

The third foundation your children need is a base of kindness. I define kindness as compassion and tenderness in action. Colossians 3:12 says, "Therefore, as God's chosen people, holy and dearly loved, clothe yourselves with compassion, kindness, humility, gentleness and patience." Most people have no problem applying that call to kindness to people *outside* the home. It's shocking to me that so many people fail to show kindness to their own families. Parents often express disappointment, judgment, harsh words, and manipulation toward their children in a way that would shock anyone else. Some parents excuse this kind of behavior by saying, "It's best for them" or "They know I really love them." But *do they*? They only know what you show them. If all you're showing them is disdain and a short temper, that's all you're *really* teaching them. When we treat other people with more care and kindness than we show our own children, we are actively undermining their sense of self-worth. Although it's probably unintentional, we are showing them with our actions that *everyone but them* is worthy of our kindness. That can destroy children's self-esteem and set them on a self-destructive path.

WHEN WE TREAT OTHER PEOPLE WITH MORE CARE AND KINDNESS THAN WE SHOW OUR OWN CHILDREN, WE ARE ACTIVELY UNDERMINING THEIR SENSE OF SELF-WORTH.

As parents, John and I tried to keep firmly in our minds the importance of treating our children with kindness. Even when we were correcting or disciplining bad behavior, we were committed to showing kindness and compassion—not to mention grace. Yes, our children are going to fail and they are going to make mistakes. Some of those failures and mistakes are going to be whoppers! But most of the time, children already know what their failures and shortcomings are. They don't need us to constantly remind them what they're *not* good at. Instead, we should focus on building up their strengths and showing them how to make the best use out of the gifts God's given them.

We also need to be mindful of what we say about our children to other people—especially when the child can hear us. John and I always tried to praise our children as much as possible in public, focusing on their strengths and the best parts of their character and personality. No child needs to hear their mom or dad gossip to others about their mistakes. That only tears them down and crushes their spirit. Your children need to know you're their biggest fan. No, I'm not saying you need to be an obnoxious cheerleader, telling everyone within earshot how great and wonderful and *special* your child is. But when you do talk about your child, do so with kindness and respect. That is such a powerful weapon against self-doubt and low self-esteem. Your children will have to make many difficult decisions as they climb their own mountains in life; do your best to send them off on the journey with the boldness and self-confidence that comes from knowing their parents believe in them.

A FOUNDATION OF FAITH

This chapter has focused on building a strong foundation for your children, but that foundation will be wholly incomplete if you don't first prepare the ground. Just as a building will crumble without a good foundation, a plant will wither and die without fertile soil. We can plant the seeds, water them, and fuss over them, but if they aren't planted in fertile ground, they'll never grow big and strong. In order for a tree to stand tall, it must put its roots deeply in the ground and draw vital nutrients from the earth below. Your children are the same way.

In the thirteenth chapter of Matthew's Gospel, Jesus tells a parable about a man planting seeds. Some fell by the wayside and were devoured by birds. Some fell into stony places where roots could not grow, so they withered away in the heat of the sun. Some fell among thorns and were choked before they could grow. None of those was a good outcome. However, some of the seeds landed in fertile soil where they grew strong and produced an abundant crop. Like those seeds, a productive life requires strong roots that grow deep into the fertile soil—the fertile soil of faith.

Psalm 1:1–3 highlights the difference between a rootless life and a life deeply rooted in faith:

Blessed is the one who does not walk in step with the wicked or stand in the way that sinners take or sit in the company of mockers, but whose delight is in the law of the LORD, *and who meditates on his law day and night. That person is like a tree planted by streams of water, which yields its fruit in season and whose leaf does not wither— whatever they do prospers.* (NKJV)

In John's Gospel, Jesus explains this principle even further:

Abide in Me, and I in you. As the branch cannot bear fruit of itself, unless it abides in the vine, neither can you, unless you abide in Me. I am the vine, you are the branches. He who abides in Me, and I in him, bears much fruit; for without Me you can do nothing. (JOHN 15:4–5, NKJV)

To *abide* means to dwell or reside. When we are born again, our *home* is Christ, and through Him, the kingdom of God. We are actually joined to Christ in a supernatural way. Acts 17:28 explains, "in Him we live and move and have our being" (NKJV).

YOUR CHILDREN WILL HAVE TO MAKE
MANY DIFFICULT DECISIONS AS THEY
CLIMB THEIR OWN MOUNTAINS IN LIFE.

He is one with the Father and we are one with Christ. By planting our faith in Jesus, we are literally rooting our lives in the very power and security of Almighty God. There can be no stronger foundation.

And yet, how often do we see parents—even Christian parents—putting their faith in other forms of security? People tend to provide stability for their children by focusing on a house, nice things, plenty of activities, trips, cars, and so on. The list of material things masquerading as security is endless. But security is not about *where* you live or *how* you live; security is about *for whom* you live. I saw this played out in a dramatic fashion when I was in high school. I had the opportunity to study for a time in Paris. Because it was a private school, most of the students who accompanied me to Paris had wealthy parents. Living so closely with them during this time allowed me to see their values in an up close and personal way. I was shocked and saddened by what I saw. The lives of many students seemed to revolve around money and possessions. As a result, their lifestyle choices challenged me. I felt pressured to "go with the flow" and follow them into some really bad decisions. After all, an entire ocean separated me from my family; they'd have no idea what I was doing. It was hard at times, but I was determined to make choices that were consistent with my faith and what my parents taught me. That was only possible because they had done such a good job making sure I was firmly rooted in my faith in Christ.

I like to contrast my time in Paris to what I experienced when John and I moved to Brazil. We were met with poverty, a foreign culture, different language, unfamiliar foods, and social norms that were far outside our experience. If my roots had been in the comforts and security of home, I would have folded like a house of cards. I would have literally been *uprooted* from everything that held me in place. However, since my foundation was in Christ, I made it through just fine. Jesus, my Rock and Foundation, was in Brazil with me. I thank God every day for parents who worked hard to make sure I had my feet planted on solid ground. Their faithfulness to God's calling gave me the best possible start in life and ensured my roots would grow deep and strong in the unmoving, unshakable bedrock of Jesus Christ.

LAUNCHING GREAT ADULTS
INTO THE WORLD

Raising godly children is not for the faint of heart. It's difficult and messy. John and I struggled a lot. We often felt battered from storms of uncertainty and confusion that hit unexpectedly as we struggled to equip our children with the roots they needed. Even when things got dark and chaotic, we knew God would see us through. We held fast to the words of David, "Even though I walk through the darkest valley, I will fear no evil, for you are with me" (Psalm 23:4). God was with us through every moment we spent in a dark valley; with our faith rooted firmly in Him, we were able to face each one with peace and hope.

THAT FIRM FOUNDATION ISN'T JUST FERTILE SOIL FOR GROWING ROOTS; IT'S A LAUNCHING PAD FOR SENDING AMAZING ADULTS OUT INTO THE WORLD.

That's the kind of depth we must provide for our children—a deep, secure foundation upon which they can "live [their] lives in him, rooted and built up in him, strengthened in the faith as [they] were taught, and overflowing with thankfulness" (Colossians 2:6–7). That firm foundation isn't just fertile soil for growing roots; it's a launching pad for sending amazing adults out into the world.

Know–Be–Live

KNOW

Take a moment to reflect on your own childhood. Think about what kind of home you grew up in, how your parents interacted with you, the lessons you learned by watching the "grownups" in your life, and so on. Looking back, what made the biggest difference in your life—both positively and negatively? What contributed most to the man or woman you've become?

_____

_____

_____

BE

In this chapter, we covered three key foundations for raising children: Be Committed, Be Consistent, and Be Kind. Think through each one and grade yourself on how well (or poorly) you're doing in each area with your children. If you are not a parent, use this opportunity to grade yourself on how well you're living up to these godly standards in your other relationships.

Be Committed

_____

_____

_____

Be Consistent

_____

_____

_____

Know–Be–Live

Be Kind

_____

_____

_____

LIVE

Now that you've assessed how you're doing in each area, it's time to set some goals for improvement. Go back through each area and set specific goals for changes you need to make. Take your time and pray through each area, noting exactly how you're going to apply commitment, consistency, and kindness in a new way.

Be Committed

_____

_____

_____

Be Consistent

_____

_____

_____

Be Kind

_____

_____

_____

CHAPTER 5

Blazing a Trail for Others to Follow

***

Your testimonies are my heritage forever,
for they are the joy of my heart.
—Psalm 119:111 (ESV)

One of my mother's favorite sayings was, "The days are long, but life is short." You can probably relate. Whether it's thinking back to your childhood, watching your own children grow up, looking back over a long career, or any other part of your life, I'm sure there were days that seemed to drag on forever. As a camp director, I heard from so many parents who struggled to fill the long summer days with activities for their children. Lack of stimulation (plus a child's rambunctiousness and short attention span) can make those hours drag by in a painful slog. But then, at the end of the summer, when it's time to send the children back to school, many parents feel a sense of loss. They think, *Where did the summer go? How did it go by so quickly?* My mother knew how. It's because the days are long, but life is short.

EVERY DAY IS A NEW OPPORTUNITY TO MAKE A DIFFERENCE—TO BLAZE A TRAIL AND LEAVE A LEGACY FOR EVERYONE YOUR LIFE TOUCHES.

It's an interesting paradox. Time can move painfully slow on a frustrating or boring day, but months and years can fly by in the blink of an eye. That means we've got to make the best use of the time we've got, because it'll be gone in an instant. The apostle Paul talked about this in his letter to the Ephesians. "Be very careful, then, how you live," he wrote, "not as unwise but as wise, making the most of every opportunity" (Ephesians 5:15–16). What Paul is talking about here is *legacy*. Every day is a new opportunity to make a difference—to blaze a trail and leave a legacy for everyone your life touches. That only happens, though, when we pay attention and look for those opportunities.

John and I have spent a lot of time thinking about our own legacy lately, and I want to pass on what we've discovered. No, this is not a chapter on estate planning and financial investments (although those are important). Rather, we think that, at the end of the day, our legacy will come down to two key areas: our legacy of influence and our legacy of family values. In this chapter, we'll dig into these and see how subtle changes now can make huge payoffs for those who follow us later.

A LEGACY OF INFLUENCE

Just a few generations ago, people usually didn't have the chance to live several years or decades after retiring. In 1921, the year my father was born, the average life expectancy was sixty for men and sixty-one for women.[6] In 2016, it was seventy-six and eighty-one, respectively.[7] That means we're living about two decades longer than we did a hundred years ago. This has brought about a new challenge for many of us: What do we do with last quarter of our lives? Once our children are grown and gone and we wrap up our careers, what does one do in these years called *retirement*?

Many look forward to this time as a peaceful reward for all their long years of hard work. They imagine days spent fishing or socializing or just sitting in a comfy chair reading a book all day. Others see these years as a time to reboot their lives and embark on brand-new adventures. Almost everyone, though, begins to think about the legacy they're going to leave behind. They get their wills together and make a plan for who gets what of their stuff.

But are our belongings the only *legacy* we leave behind? Having been the recipient of my parents' lifetime of wisdom, grace, faithfulness, love, generosity, time, and experience, I would emphatically

---

6 "Life expectancy in the USA, 1900-1998," University of California-Berkeley, accessed June 11, 2018, http://www.demog.berkeley.edu/~andrew/1918/figure2.html).

7 "Mortality in the United States, 2016," NCHS Data Brief (No. 293), Centers for Disease Control and Prevention, December, 2017, https://www.cdc.gov/nchs/data/databriefs/db293.pdf.

say *no*. Financial assets are important and you certainly need a plan for managing those after your death. However, your true legacy isn't *just* about your money. In fact, it's not even *mainly* about your money. The legacy you'll leave *then* is the life you're living *now*. Your legacy doesn't happen later; it's happening right now. It doesn't matter how old (or young) you are—you are *already* blazing a trail for others to follow. That trail is your influence.

KINGDOM INFLUENCE

My mother always kept a little framed excerpt of the poem "Only One Life" by C.T. Studd sitting on her kitchen counter. I must have read it a hundred times in my life, and the poem's refrain, which is repeated eight times in the piece, is always ringing in my ears:

> Only one life, t'will soon be past,
> Only what's done for Christ will last.

"Only what's done for Christ" will live on into eternity, impacting generation after generation. Only a life filled with the fruit of the spirit—love, joy, peace, patience, kindness, goodness, faithfulness, gentleness, and self-control (Galatians 5:22–23)—will influence family members, friends, and strangers, because that life will make a *kingdom* impact. The message of salvation through Christ is a treasure beyond telling that can, will, and has change(d) the world. It is His story we proclaim, His life we pass along, and the knowledge of His inestimable gifts we pass to our families and future generations. This is true legacy; this is an inheritance worthy of His name.

FAMILY INFLUENCE

You can never overestimate the impact you're having on your family. Walking with a parent, spouse, child, or sibling every single day throughout your entire life leaves an unmistakable, undeniable mark on your heart. Those experiences—positive *and* negative—have molded you into the man or woman you are today, just as you are currently molding others around you. This truth came into sharp focus for me when I lost my parents. Mom and Dad died within ten months of each other in 2014–2015. They each lived amazing lives that continued into their nineties, but the weight of that loss was hard to bear. After going through the painful, almost endless hours of cleaning out their home—a place in which they lived for fifty-eight years—I found myself sifting through reminders of the tremendous impact they had on my life. I understood in that moment that the most precious things they left me were our shared memories and their influence.

THE LEGACY YOU'LL LEAVE THEN IS THE LIFE YOU'RE LIVING NOW.

I'm so grateful for the heritage of godly parents whose lives were built on biblical principles with outstanding ethics, morals, and values consistently on display to those around them. They left an indelible mark on my life and on the lives of their grandchildren and great-grandchildren. Right after my mother passed away, our grandchildren continued to talk about her life. Though they were young at the time, they realized she prayed for them and with them; she supported and encouraged them. Without a doubt, they knew she cared deeply for them. Those memories and the incredible gift of being valued and respected by such a precious soul is a legacy worth more than any worldly treasure. Her influence will be felt throughout untold generations of her family and every life they touch.

Because my parents focused their lives on *influence* rather than *affluence*, I have come to recognize the legacy I am living for my children and grandchildren. Regardless how long or short my time is here on earth, I want the way I live my life to be a gift, something I *donate* to my family and friends every single day. I don't want to miss a single opportunity to influence and impact their lives for the better.

EVERYDAY INFLUENCE

John worked for the International Mission Board for twenty years. Leaving there after such a long, meaningful tenure was a big deal for us, and the decision to move on wasn't an easy one. However, we each felt the Lord shifting our focus into other areas of influence. For years we had worked to be wise stewards of our time, talents, and resources, but we had never stopped to consider what it meant to be a good steward of our influence. We were curious to see how and where He'd use us next. Needless to say, we were a little surprised to discover that the new mission field He had prepared for us was right outside our front door. We began to see every interaction, every situation as an opportunity to share our influence.

Some of those opportunities, of course, are small and simple. For instance, if you smile at a perfect stranger, you can almost always get them to smile back; this is influence. If you nod and say, "Good morning," to someone walking towards you on the sidewalk, most of the time, they will respond with a greeting of their own; this is influence. In both situations, as trivial as they may appear, you're doing something significant: you're telling someone that you *see* them. You're acknowledging them as a person, as a human being who has dignity and who deserves your kindness and attention. It's sobering to think about how many people in the world do not believe that about themselves. We're surrounded by people who are literally starving for attention, but attention is one of the quickest and easiest gifts we have to give!

Other opportunities can make a much bigger impact on many more people. For example, if my brother Dan, who is the CEO of

Chick-fil-A, calls and asks for my advice on a work matter, that one conversation could impact more than forty thousand employees and millions of customers. Likewise, authors, speakers, artists, leaders, pastors, and other professionals influence dozens or thousands of people regularly. And, as we've seen in recent years, a single Twitter post from a "regular person" can become national news in a heartbeat. We have more ways to spread our influence to more people than ever before. That's a responsibility none of us should take for granted.

A LEGACY OF FAMILY VALUES

Going through my mother's things after she died was indeed a difficult task, but it was one filled with immense joy for me. Touching the things she had touched, going through boxes of memories, and looking at countless old photographs solidified my view of her as a steady, faithful woman of God. There is no doubt that her life will reverberate through her children, her grandchildren, her great-grandchildren, and beyond for generations to come. My parents understood that their time on earth was precious—and they refused to waste it. Beyond leaving a financial and business legacy behind them, they were passionate about setting a godly example for their children and building strong, resilient homes that honored God. They did so by demonstrating and living by our core family values.

Being effective in life means knowing what is important and having a clear focus on the principles that guide your decision-making process. Those things make up your *values*, and living according to your God-given values will give your life meaning and impact that will still be here long after you're gone. While different values may be important to different families, I've found these three principles to be fairly consistent among our Christian friends:

1. Family values articulate our calling.
2. Family values inform our actions.
3. Family values create family traditions.

Let's break these down a bit.

FAMILY VALUES ARTICULATE OUR CALLING

John and I take family values very seriously, and throughout our marriage we have developed a list of five values we believe encapsulates God's call on our family. Those values are Faith, Family, Integrity, Generosity, and Gratitude. Not a week went by in our children's lives when they didn't hear us emphasize one or all of these values. We believed these five things defined who we were as a family. Going back to the theme of the previous chapter, we also prayed that these five values would provide the most fertile soil in which our children' roots could grow deep, giving them a strong foundation.

I'm happy to say that our prayers were answered. All four of our children have grown into wonderful adults and all four of them now have spouses and children of their own. As they left home and started their families, John and I encouraged them to take what they learned from us and establish their own family values. We weren't interested in having them copy what John and I had come up with so many years ago. Instead, we wanted them to pray with their spouses about who they each wanted to be as families and about the key lessons they wanted to be sure to impart to their children. Having been raised in a family that freely and often discussed their values, they each developed a list of values that guide their decisions and behaviors as a family:

- Joy (daughter) and Trent: Generosity, Fear of God, Joy, Compassion, Hospitality, and Gratitude
- John (son) and Kylie: Humility, Gratitude, Generosity, Faith, and Family/Relationships

- Angela (daughter) and Brent: Faith, Generosity, Authentic Community, Compassion, and Humility
- David (son) and Ashley: Generosity, Accountability, Compassion, Patience, and Family

We've created a collage of all five families' values that hangs in our home. It's a constant reminder that we are men and women with a calling. God has a purpose for each of us and for each of our families, and we are determined to live out that purpose to the best of our ability.

FAMILY VALUES INFORM OUR ACTIONS

Each of the values I've listed—mine and John's and those of our children's families—are grounded in our relationships with God. Proverbs 9:10 says, "The fear of the LORD is the beginning of wisdom, and knowledge of the Holy One is understanding." The word translated as *fear* in this verse is the Hebrew word *yirah*, which literally means an extreme reverence for and recognition of God's ultimate greatness. By focusing on Him, I believe God has given us a taste of His wisdom, which we've used to guide our actions and decisions. To be clear, this wisdom is 100 percent a gift from God; it's not something we could ever earn or deserve on our own. As James explains, "If any of you lacks wisdom, you should ask God, who gives generously to all without finding fault, and it will be given to you" (James 1:5). That means godly wisdom is a gift God freely pours out onto those who earnestly seek Him. This is a powerful gift, as James continues, "The wisdom that is from above is first pure, then peaceable, gentle, willing to yield, full of mercy and good fruits, without partiality and without hypocrisy" (James 3:17, NKJV).

We put that wisdom to use in our decision-making, first in choosing what our family values should be and then in using those values to inform our actions. The collage in our home is an invaluable tool for this because it constantly refocuses our thoughts onto what we've said is important to us. Whenever we're faced with an opportunity, challenge, or any other decision, we can look to our family values for some direction on how we should proceed. In that way, our values serve as guardrails, informing our actions and keeping us from getting off course. For example, one of our family values is Generosity. Giving is important to our family, and we always want to be conduits of the blessings we've received. So whenever an opportunity to give comes up, our values demand that we at least consider it. Sure, we may decide against giving to a particular cause or organization, but we never dismiss these things blindly. We filter those opportunities through the wisdom God's granted us, and then we try to make the best decision. As a family, we want all our decisions, big and small, to honor Him.

Another one of our values is Family. I was blessed to have parents who shared this value. Each year when I was growing up, my parents took our family on a trip during Thanksgiving break. Over the years, we went to Miami, tropical islands, Mexico City, and even to some overseas locales. We have so many memories of those times together. Acting silly and playing games while riding in the car, sharing stories and singing together while traveling, even fussing occasionally as siblings do—these are some of my happiest memories. Even when our vacations weren't especially fancy or elaborate (most weren't), my parents went out of their way to create memories for me and my brothers that have lasted a lifetime. That's the kind of priorities you set if you make Family one of your values, and that's the kind of intentional life you lead when you align your actions with your values.

FAMILY VALUES CREATE FAMILY TRADITIONS

Your family values should center on what's most important for you, your spouse, and your children. They identify who you are and what you aspire to be as a family. That's what makes these values so personal, so intimately connected to each family. There is no cookie-cutter formula that works for everyone, so I would never dream of telling you what values you should select. It is 100 percent up to you. I would encourage you as you begin to establish your family values, though, to spend plenty of time thinking, talking, and praying about your selections. Don't rush it. Whatever you set as a family value will deserve—even demand—your time, attention, and money. If you aren't willing to actually follow through with the nitty-gritty of the values you set, don't put it on the list. Your family values shouldn't answer, *What if we?* Instead, they should perfectly crystalize, *Who are we?* When you know who you are as a family, what's important to you will come into focus.

Once you have that list of values in hand, and once you start intentionally building your life around these things, something interesting happens. You'll notice that your family starts to fall into certain patterns. Over time, these patterns will likely turn into the family traditions that will live on in the hearts and minds of your children forever. For example, you may select Service as a family value. To model that value, you might volunteer your family to serve Christmas dinner at the local homeless shelter one year. Remembering how that act of service impacted your children, you do the same thing the following year. One year becomes two. Two becomes five. Five becomes ten. Without even realizing it or forcing it from the outset, you've created a meaningful family tradition of service at Christmas. For the rest of their lives, your children will remember those special times every year during the holidays. They may even continue the tradition with their own families, taking the act of service you started into a new generation.

John and I have seen so many of our most beloved family traditions spring out of our values. Early on, we set a family value of Family. That means we are intentional about structuring our time, attention, and money around building wonderful, relationship-building experiences for our marriage, our children, and our grandchildren. One of those traditions is something we call

Swaddling Clothes. When our children were young, they always wanted to open gifts on Christmas Eve. John and I wanted to save most of the magic for Christmas morning, but one year I came up with a compromise. I bought each child a new pair of special pajamas, washed and wrapped them, and put them under the tree. Then, when the unavoidable begging began on Christmas Eve, I told them they could open one present of my choosing. However, before they could open the gift, I shared each one's birth story. I emphasized to each child how special they were and how much of a gift they were to John and me. Then I read part of the Christmas story, highlighting Mary's pregnancy and how excited and scared she must have been before Jesus's birth. I also focused on the description of Jesus in Luke 2:2 as being "wrapped in swaddling clothes." Then I let the children open the gift I picked out for them—their new pajamas—and they ran off to put them on for the night. Seeing the children greet Christmas morning in those special pajamas moved me in an unexpected way. I was reminded of Psalm 127:3, "Children are a heritage from the LORD, offspring a reward from him." Truly, each child is a gift straight from God! We repeated our *Swaddling Clothes* tradition the next year, and then the next. To this day, whoever is able to come to our house on Christmas Eve receives a new pair of pajamas after a special time of sharing. It has become a family tradition that my children, and now my grandchildren, cherish as part of the holidays.

Another tradition that has grown out of our Family value is something we call *Family Assembly*. Once our children married and started families of their own, John and I quickly realized how much we missed the long conversations and quality time we used to have with our children on a daily basis. We adore our grandchildren, of course, but having them around every time we see our children changes the whole dynamic. It became impossible to finish a conversation or have an uninterrupted visit with our adult children when their little ones were running around. Instead of simply accepting this change as a natural part of life, John and I looked to our Family value and came up with a solution. We started planning an annual, adults-only long weekend for us with our children and their spouses. No little children allowed! John and I always offer to pay for babysitting and travel expenses if necessary because we don't want any excuses. This guarantees that we have plenty of time to engage with our children and sons- and daughters-in-law as adults. Our conversations are richer than they'd be with children in the mix, and we don't have to worry about interruptions or watching the clock. We can be fully present with one another. We've gone away on these *Family Assembly* weekends every year for more than a decade, and it's become one of my and John's favorite times of the year.

We've grown to love this dedicated time with our children so much that we've recently started a similar yearly tradition focused on our grandchildren—fifteen and counting! John and I plan an entire weekend in the summer that we call Camp MiPa—a play on words based on what the grandchildren call us. We plan these long weekends like a mini-Vacation Bible School, complete with a theme, Bible lessons, songs, and plenty of recreation. This is a great way for us to make connections with our grandchildren and to reinforce their connections between their cousins. When John and I are long gone, we want this generation to remember us fondly, remember the Bible lessons we discussed, and remain intimately connected with one another. The bonds of family and faith are critical, and we will do everything we can to make sure our grandchildren are strongly rooted in both. Of course, we also want to build personal relationships with each grandchild individually. That's why, in addition to Camp MiPa, we've also committed to take each grandson and granddaughter on special birthday trips every three years from age eight to age seventeen. This gives us one-on-one time with each one, so we can stay plugged in to their lives and make sure we continue to get to know the fine young men and women they are becoming.

These are just a few examples of how one of our family values, Family, has spawned several traditions that we cherish. Your family traditions will be different; sometimes you can intentionally create them like we did with *Family Assembly*, and other times you'll just fall into them naturally like we did with *Swaddling Clothes*. Either way, the goal should be to solidify the legacy you're leaving by creating memories and sharing experiences with the people you hold near and dear. Our children and grandchildren won't remember every single conversation we've had during these special trips and weekends, but they will never forget how important each one of them is to us.

LIVING LEGACIES

In today's world, we often hear about *living legends*. This is used to describe everyone from music stars to philanthropists. We hear the phrase so often that it's practically lost its meaning; overuse has stripped it of its impact. I'd like to suggest an alternative in the context of this chapter. I don't know about you, but I don't really want to be a *legend*. A generation from now, I don't want people to wonder whether or not I was really here or to speculate on the impact I had on the world. I'd rather them *see* that impact alive and well even after I'm gone. That kind of enduring mark on the world doesn't come from a legend; it comes from a legacy. You can keep your *living legends*. I'd rather be a *living legacy*.

The value of living a legacy cannot be overstated. It is a treasure we leave "where moths and vermin do not destroy, and where thieves do not break in and steal" (Matthew 6:20). Unlike material wealth that can only be left to a few, a living legacy can be bequeathed to every single person your life touches. A living legacy is a lifestyle; it is a moment-by-moment choice to make "the most of every opportunity" (Ephesians 5:16). Just as mountains are climbed one step at a time, so it is with leaving a living legacy. Not only do we have the joy of knowing God's mercies are new every morning (Lamentations 3:22–23), we can rest assured that His mercy is renewed each moment of every day. When we fail in one moment, we have the next to make a better, godlier choice.

JUST AS MOUNTAINS ARE CLIMBED ONE STEP AT A TIME, SO IT IS WITH LEAVING A LIVING LEGACY.

Becoming a living legacy isn't always easy. It is an epic climb that will take time and focus. Every moment of your life will contribute to the legacy you're living now and leaving behind. But those moments add up. They blaze a trail that others can follow. They cut a path up the mountain that will guide those coming after you and help make their journey a little easier.

Know–Be–Live

KNOW

In what ways are you currently living a legacy of influence and family values? Be specific, and don't let yourself off the hook if you're falling short in either area. Honestly evaluate the intentional impact you are having on those around you today.

_____

_____

_____

_____

_____

_____

BE

What behaviors, habits, attitudes, or commitments need to change in order for you to more effectively live the kind of legacy-building life God's calling you to live?

_____

_____

_____

_____

_____

_____

Know–Be–Live

LIVE

With these things in mind, start two separate lists. First, start listing the specific ways you can begin influencing those around you. How can you use your influence to improve their lives (and your own), as well as better serve the Lord? Second, start a list of potential family values that reflect who you are as a family. Remember, these should state who you are and who you realistically want to be. Do not put anything on this list if you aren't willing to follow through with the hard work of putting it into practice. Discuss these options with your family and narrow them down to three to five family values that you can live by for the rest of your lives.

CHAPTER 6
Trials of the Trail

—❧≈❧—

Cast your cares on the LORD *and he will sustain you.*
—PSALM 55:22

So far in this book, we've talked about different parts of the journey we all take up the mountains of life. We discussed starting the journey by embracing our identity in Christ. Then we talked about how to build momentum by becoming good stewards of the many gifts God's given (and entrusted to) us. We accepted the challenge to scale to new heights of significance by identifying what God wants us to do and how to better listen for His direction. We saw that we aren't alone on the journey, as we're called to equip our children and blaze a trail for others to follow. At this point, I'd love to congratulate you and welcome you to the summit. I'd love to give you a big hug and tell you that you've arrived. I'd really love to do that. But I can't.

The truth is, we're only halfway up the mountain. We still have a few critical steps to cover in this book—and they are the most unwelcome parts of the journey. I'm talking about what I call the *trials of the trail*, the challenges we all face as we climb. The journey we're taking isn't some picture-perfect, idealized straight line from start to finish. It's not pain-free, stress-free, or worry-free. Sometimes, the road is hard. The path before us is often blocked. At times, we realize we've been traveling down the wrong road and have to backtrack. Those moments are never easy, but they are always—*always*—part of the journey. Remember, Jesus assured us that we would face trials and hardships in life. He said, "In this world you will have trouble" (John 16:33). Trouble is not a *possibility* in life; it is a *certainty*. The good news we must remember in times of pain, though, is that He has already secured the victory for us. He continues, "But take heart! I have overcome the world" (John 16:33). He *already* sees us on top of the mountain. He knows how to get us there. That doesn't mean, however, that we can bypass all adversity as we travel. In fact, the best way to get *to* the destination is often to go *through* the difficulties standing in our way.

Over the next few chapters, we're going to face some of those difficulties—specifically, we'll discuss adversity and sickness (this chapter), getting older (chapter 7), and experiencing grief (chapter 8). As we get started, though, I want to be clear right off the bat. We could never solve the problems of pain and sickness in one book, let alone one or two chapters. Pain is real, and it is often heartbreaking. If you're going through a season of hardship right now, I'd never dream of making light of your struggle by offering simple, trite, cheery, and ultimately unhelpful solutions to your pain. Though well-intentioned, these things can compound the pain our friends are feeling. It can make them feel like a failure for *allowing* the pain to hurt so much. We want to be a blessing when our loved ones are hurting, and we can't bless someone by making them feel guilty for their grief.

So what are we to do? I think the answer is community. Pain always seems harder to bear when we try to bear it alone. Therefore I want to encourage you to walk with those who are hurting and to seek out the support of others when you are facing a mountain of hardship yourself. We can overcome together what we could never overcome alone. Of course, we can also search Scripture for God's assurances in the midst of our pain. To do that, I want to share some very personal stories of my own family's journey up the mountain of physical sickness and tell you what we learned. My prayer is that, by giving you a window into my family's experiences, I can show you that you are not alone in whatever pain you're going through.

OUR BODIES MATTER TO GOD

Health is a wonderful gift from the Lord. God's Word tells us that we are fearfully and wonderfully made; every cell in our bodies was crafted with care (Psalm 139:14–16). When Adam and Eve were in the Garden, there was no sickness—no health concerns whatsoever. Can you imagine that? They had all they needed for a full and healthy life. Everything was just as God wanted it to be. And then, the moment sin entered the world, people began to experience difficulty, disease, sorrow, and death.

Not only are we fearfully and wonderfully made, but Romans 12:1 teaches us that our physical bodies are to be cared for as a living sacrifice, holy and devoted to God: "Therefore, I urge you, brothers and sisters, in view of God's mercy, to offer your bodies as a living sacrifice, holy and pleasing to God—this is your true and proper worship." God calls us to care for the bodies He made for us by giving ourselves adequate rest, proper nutrition, and regular exercise. By doing these things, we are honoring God and showing ourselves to be wise stewards of the gift of life He's given us.

The Bible also tells us that our bodies, if we choose to follow Christ, are temples of His Holy Spirit, the place where God dwells. First Corinthians 6:19–20 says, "Do you not know that your bodies are temples of the Holy Spirit, who is in you, whom you have received from God? You are not your own; you were bought at a price. Therefore honor God with your bodies." He is ever-present, always with us—*within* us. He not only resides within us, He also shows Himself and demonstrates His power *through* us. Isaiah 61:3 declares, "They will be called oaks of righteousness, a planting of the LORD for the display of his splendor." Can there be a better compliment to the human body than to be used as a "display of His splendor"?

Clearly, our bodies are important to God. They weren't an afterthought or simply designed as a wrapper for our eternal spirits. That may be why it is so hard for us to comprehend the physical pain and suffering we see around us or experience ourselves. We see and feel the weakness of the body and can't help but wonder what's going on. I can't give you an easy answer for that. Over the years and through plenty of firsthand experience, though, I've learned that God never wastes an opportunity; He certainly never intends the pain we face in our lives to be wasted. There are lessons to be learned even in the darkest circumstances. At least in my experience, the lesson He most often drives home in my weakness is His unyielding commitment to mold me into the faithful woman of God He wants me to be. He'll use any situation to remind me that

GOD NEVER WASTES AN OPPORTUNITY;
THERE ARE LESSONS TO BE LEARNED EVEN
IN THE DARKEST CIRCUMSTANCES.

He's in charge, not me. I've found that God is much more concerned with my character than my comfort, and He'll use any and all circumstances to shape my character into a better reflection of His Son. Romans 8:28 makes this clear, "And we know that in all things God works for the good of those who love him, who have been called according to his purpose." Those may not be comforting words in the throes of anguish, but the truth remains: God will use any situation for His glory and for your good.

ENTERING THE VALLEY OF THE SHADOW OF DEATH

As I said before, I don't simply want to tell you what you should do and learn in your suffering. Instead, I think the best thing I can do is to give you a glimpse at some of the hard lessons I've learned by walking through a few of my darkest valleys. As I begin this story, I'm reminded of the magnificent 23rd Psalm. There, David writes about facing and conquering his own hardships. It's truly one of the most beautifully written passages in the whole Bible. What resonates with me most now is verse 4, "Yea, though I walk through the valley of the shadow of death, I will fear no evil; For You are with me; Your rod and Your staff, they comfort me" (NKJV). A few years ago, I became intimately acquainted with the "valley of the shadow of death." In fact, I felt like death's shadow was looming all around me. I got the worst news I could imagine: my husband—my best friend and partner for life—was sick.

John went to the doctor for a routine checkup in the spring of 2014. He hadn't been feeling sick and didn't have any obvious signs of a problem, so we were blindsided by the doctor's report: John had prostate cancer. The mention of *cancer* terrified me. After many long, detailed discussions with the doctor and others, we opted for surgery. As we were still reeling from the diagnosis and planning for the surgery, John's father unexpectedly passed away. Just three days before his surgery, John and I found ourselves in the middle of a family tragedy. We traveled to his mother's house to support her in her grief, help the family take care of the arrangements, and plan and attend the memorial service.

Needless to say, there were times during that month when I felt overwhelmed. John had lost his father and was facing a health crisis of his own. My mother-in-law had lost her husband—and I was worried about losing mine. God taught me a critical lesson during this season of hardship: When you don't know what to do, do what you *do* know to do. For us, that meant keeping our eyes focused on the Lord. We chose to trust Jesus and His promise to be our source of strength and peace. The pain was real and our flesh was weak, but Jesus did not let us down. The surgery was successful, John began his road to recovery, and we were confident that the cancer battle was over.

We were wrong.

Three years later, the cancer returned. This time, we faced eight long weeks of five radiation treatments per week. John was only in his late fifties and I couldn't imagine life without him, but we had to prepare for the worst. If we were facing death, we needed to be ready. This meant making sure our wills were up-to-date, purchasing cemetery plots, selecting our coffins, and making basic arrangements with our children. It also meant I had to learn some new skills and prepare for new responsibilities. Up until that point, John had taken care of paying our monthly bills; I began to take over this process just in case the task became mine permanently. We had intentional conversations that would help me if I was to be left a widow. These were obviously hard topics of conversation, but they were necessary. Through this difficult season, we learned that times of hardship can bring even the closest couples closer together. Looking back, I can see that this journey is not a path we would have chosen for ourselves, but it heightened our sensitivity and appreciation for each other. I can truly say I'm thankful God had us walk that season together.

One month after his final radiation treatment, we received news that John was once again cancer-free. We praised God for this wonderful report, for choosing to extend his time on earth. We also thanked Him as we recognized we were not the same for having walked this road together. Trials have a way of transforming life. God uses difficult situations to teach us about Him. He uses circumstances to shape our character and to strengthen our trust in Him. God uses all things, all circumstances, for His glory.

I kept a private journal of my thoughts and prayers throughout John's many weeks of radiation. I never planned on showing these entries to anyone when I wrote them, but I feel led to share a few with you here. Looking back over them after a few years reminds me of the journey God led us through—and how He remained faithful even when my strength failed.

Day #4: Emotions seem "heavy" mostly because of the unknown. I'm
         thankful to cast all my cares on the Lord, b/c I'm confident

He cares for me. Prayer: You are my God, earnestly, I seek you; I thirst for you, my whole being longs for you.

Day #7: Beginning to recognize the same people coming in for their treatments. I'm finding myself drawn to pray for those who sit in here. Some are all alone. I'm thankful to walk this journey with John whether convenient or inconvenient. It's good to affirm my commitment to him when we married, in sickness or in health . . . "I do."

Day #9: Yesterday, a man sat by me waiting on his wife. She is getting both radiation and chemo treatments. They stay at the Hope Lodge in the Atlanta area and return home each weekend, only to find grass to cut, bills to pay, etc. He told me they are both so very tired. Prayer: Lord, meet the needs of this dear couple. Give them a sense of your hope today. Give him patience and love as he cares for his wife. Sustain them today!

Day #11: Whether in suffering or success, in strength or weakness, in greatness or defeat . . . His grace sustains. He gives the victory!

Day #12: Finding today to be hard, not for John but for me. Getting up, getting dressed, going downtown over and over, eventually, seems tiring. Prayer: Please let me be John's #1 supporter. Let me keep my eyes fixed on you. Give us laughter in this journey, joy along the way, increased faith in You for whatever the future holds.

Day #38: The end, it's now in sight. The days have really been long. But thank you God. You have used our children and our friends

to offer so much support through prayers, text, cards, calls,
words of encouragement and promises from Your Word.
Today, I cling to Deuteronomy 31:8, The Lord himself goes
before you and will be with you; He will never leave you nor
forsake you. Do not be afraid; do not be discouraged. I will not
leave you nor forsake you.

FACING A LOSING HEALTH BATTLE

John's recovery is a blessing for which I will never stop praising God.
It's easy to thank God and to see His goodness when we get the
outcome we want. It's much harder when we get the outcome we
don't. I faced that mountain as I watched cancer attack the other
significant man in my life—my father. He was diagnosed with cancer
of the mouth at the age of ninety-two. Following surgery to remove
a portion of his jaw, Dad's health gradually failed over the course
of one very long year. Even with round-the-clock nursing care, he
grew weaker by the day. This man who loved God and His people,
enjoyed conversations and laughter, worked his entire life, and made
bold, biblical, God-fearing decisions about his business struggled
severely and seemed to disappear before our eyes. My mom, his wife
of almost sixty-six years, and all our family were forced to look on as
he became completely helpless. He died at home surrounded by his
family on September 8, 2014, at the age of ninety-three.

Less than a year later, I watched my mother face a different
kind of health battle. She had her first heart attack years earlier
in 2001, but with the encouragement from her cardiologist and
quite a bit of determination on Mom's part to stay healthy, she
rallied. She walked three miles every day on the treadmill in her
home and did all she could to reclaim her health. Fourteen years
later, though, she developed an annoying, persistent cough. She
was ninety-two at the time. We discovered the cough was due to a

small leak in an artery, and her only hope for recovery was a risky surgical procedure. In fact, the surgeon had never attempted this particular procedure on anyone near her age. My mother looked the doctor in the eye and said, "Well, let's do whatever will help *you* the most. If you want to try this procedure on me, that will be just fine. I'm not worried about what will happen to me." Right there in that doctor's office, I saw a boldness in my mother like I had never witnessed before. She did not know *what* her future would hold but she certainly knew *Who* held her future. She was admitted to the hospital but never made it to surgery. I was holding her hand on July 22, 2015, when she passed from this earth into eternal life.

Losing both Mom and Dad within ten months of each other was a crushing blow. Yet I feel a resounding sense of confidence and hope because one day I will see them again. God's Word tells us that, as believers, we will live forever. Death will not be the end. One day our hearts will stop beating, but that is not the end of our spirits. There is so much more, because He lives in us. "The Spirit of God, who raised Jesus from the dead, lives in you. And just as God raised Christ Jesus from the dead, he will give life to your mortal bodies by this same Spirit living within you" (Romans 8:11, NLT).

Mom and Dad believed in Jesus and received His gift of eternal life; death for them was not leaving home—it was a homecoming! Because of the love of Jesus Christ, because of His death and His resurrection, my parents are more alive today than ever before.

LIVING WITH A THORN IN THE FLESH

Physical trials come and go for most of us. For some, however, the path up the mountain is never-ending. Our son David is one of those whose struggle is continuous; each step is uphill as he navigates life with his own version of what the apostle Paul called his "thorn in the flesh" (2 Corinthians 12:7).

David is our fourth child; he was born in Rio de Janeiro while John and I were missionaries in Brazil. Labor was induced as planned and nothing indicated this birth would be any different than our other three. However, the moment I delivered David, it was frighteningly obvious that something serious was wrong. Our baby boy was a deep, dark purple and his tiny body was limp and lifeless—he couldn't breathe. As the medical team worked on our son, I felt myself going into shock. John took my head in his hands and whispered repeatedly, "The LORD is our Shepherd; we shall not want. The LORD is our Shepherd; we shall not want. The LORD is our Shepherd; we shall not want" (Psalm 23:1, paraphrased).

The next thing I recall is waking up in a hospital room with John standing beside me. He gently explained our baby boy, whom we named David, had been unable to breathe on his own for nearly thirty minutes. He had suffered lack of oxygen to his brain, experienced two seizures, and had been given an Apgar score of 1.[8] He needed critical, specialized care, so David and I were taken by ambulance to a different hospital equipped to handle infants with life-threatening conditions. It had only been a few hours since giving birth, and the jostle of the ambulance caused me quite a bit of discomfort. Then the ambulance turned onto a cobblestone road that led up the side of a mountain. That's right—another mountain to mark a significant moment of my life. I felt every bump in the road deep in my being—physically and emotionally. The climb up the mountain was one filled with pain, uncertainty, despair, confusion, and doubt; it was a climb that begged for a miracle. I wondered if life would ever again be *normal*.

When we arrived at the hospital, I was admitted and David was taken immediately to the NICU. There were so many tubes and

---

8 Apgar is a test given to newborns twice—once at one minute after birth and again at five minutes after birth. The test rates a baby's Appearance (skin color), Pulse (heart rate), Grimace (reflex irritability), Activity (muscle tone), and Respiration. The highest score is 10 (two points for each assessment).

wires attached to our tiny son and so many doctors surrounding him that we could barely see him, let alone touch him. In fact, we were not allowed to hold David at all because his life was so very fragile. The hours were long and difficult as we waited for updates on his progress. Thirty-six hours later, it seemed David might be strong enough for John and me to hold him for the first time. My excitement was short-lived, as I suddenly felt weak with excruciating pain in my abdominal area.

A hurried sonogram revealed that I was bleeding internally. I had already lost a tremendous amount of blood before being rushed into an emergency hysterectomy. As my newborn infant fought for his life in another room, my own life was suddenly in jeopardy. Poor John could do nothing but pray for his family as doctors worked on both me and David. Those prayers were answered, as both patients made it through those critical days. We discovered that my condition had been far more serious than we knew, but God brought me through the surgery. Weak and shaken, I was discharged a week later.

David, however, spent more than three weeks in the hospital before he was strong enough for us to bring him home. His pediatrician made it clear to us that, due to the oxygen deprivation he had suffered, David would likely be deficient in his ability to speak, see, and walk. We prepared for the worst but clung desperately to the quiet confidence that God would sustain us. Whatever the future held in store for us, bringing our son home was a glorious day and such a celebration for our family!

When David was six months old, we took him to the United States for tests and in-depth evaluation. Following home visits and a battery of tests, the consensus was, "This can't possibly be the same child as the one who experienced a traumatic delivery!" David's coordination was normal; his vision and hearing were excellent; his fine motor skills were developing right on track. The doctors couldn't explain why David had no obvious ill effects from his extended lack of oxygen. John and I knew the explanation, though—God's healing power had brought about a miracle for our youngest son.

Not only did David develop as a completely normal little boy, he excelled in incredible ways. By the time he was four years old, we could tell he was fascinated with music. He would sit playing melodies of his favorite childhood songs for hours. At age five, he learned to play the violin. In middle school, he mastered the French horn and taught himself to play the saxophone. In fact, he had received his first saxophone for Christmas and immediately started playing "Amazing Grace." At the age of nine, David took on the lead role in *Amahl and the Night Visitors* (a Christmas opera about three kings who visit a young, crippled boy) and performed this enormous role flawlessly. There is no doubt that David is amazingly gifted. He has far exceeded any expectations his doctors had given us when he was born. He was—and still is—our miracle baby!

As David grew, however, we started seeing some signs that something was a little . . . *off*. He seemed to be forgetful a lot, which we often mistook for irresponsibility. He would continually forget his belongings, fail to remember repeated messages or directions, and was uncertain of where to go or when to be there. He also seemed to be unable to recall everyday occurrences or events. Though his forgetfulness was frustrating at times (for him and for us), David did well in high school and went on to major in music in college. He was highly intelligent, witty, creative, remarkable with his musical abilities, and determined to gain independence during his college years.

David graduated from college but found himself struggling after graduation. John and I, along with our whole family, walked with him through some dark, difficult days. This led to hours of counseling and a series of evaluations. A multitude of questions were answered when tests revealed David has developmental amnesia—a severe impairment of episodic memory. The oxygen deprivation David experienced at birth damaged an area of his brain called the hippocampus—an important part of the brain for memory storage. His hippocampus operates at only 50 percent and, to this day, he struggles when following a series of instructions or recalling what he has repeatedly heard or seen. It's hard to imagine the problems and constant frustration of knowing part of your brain is only working at half capacity.

Despite these difficulties, David is a walking miracle and a daily display of God's divine intervention. He has never known what it is to have unhampered recall; to him, his condition is normal. Even though he regularly faces embarrassing moments, challenges with day-to-day circumstances, and uneasiness in new situations, David presses on in life. He's married with one daughter, and he's a fantastic husband and father. He is self-employed, running his own carpentry business in Atlanta. He is successfully learning to navigate life while accepting his developmental amnesia, and he takes every opportunity to use his talent and skills to serve others.

We all face struggles, and some challenges, like David's, are daily. But Luke 1:37 tells us that "*With God, nothing shall be impossible*" (KJV). I strongly believe God uses all things for His glory, even our trials in life. We can do all things through Christ, who gives us strength for even the toughest uphill climbs (Philippians 4:13). David is a constant, living reminder of my mother's motto: "You can—*with God*."

FINDING HIS STRENGTH IN OUR WEAKNESS

Physical trial can truly be like a fire burning through our lives; it brings pain and devastation. We can be so overwhelmed by illness or disability that we shout at the heavens, asking God why He would allow these things to happen. It can seem as though He has turned away from us and left us in despair. But that is not the character of our God. He is never uninvolved in or apathetic to what we face. When we hurt, He hurts. When we cry, He holds every tear. Rather than asking Him *why* we face trials, let us instead strive to ask *what* He wishes to teach us through the trial. He wants to teach us and mold us into the best possible version of ourselves. He wants to purify us as gold through a refiner's fire. In His ultimate wisdom, God chooses *what* we go through in life. But we choose *how* we go through it.

The moment when we are at our weakest is the very moment we most need to reach toward our Lord. He promises in Hebrews 13:5, "Never will I leave you; never will I forsake you." He also promises to be our strength when our strength is gone: "My grace is sufficient for you, for my power is made perfect in weakness" (2 Corinthians 12:9). We see this same truth in Isaiah 40:29, "He gives strength to the weary and increases the power of the weak."

Over the years, my family has scaled a few particularly rugged mountains of physical trial. These hardships seemed momentous to us, but I know no family is immune to sickness. In fact, I have been amazed by the strength and confidence with which many of my friends have powered through what appeared from the outside to be an insurmountable obstacle. Some of my most humbling moments have come watching others face terrible adversity and physical pain with relentless and unwavering faith. It seems no matter how horrible the situation, their faith would not be shaken. I love seeing God show up and show off in the most difficult circumstances. No matter how grueling the trials we face, He is guiding each step of the way. Our God is always in control. When His children acknowledge His omnipotence, He receives all the honor and glory and we see Him for who He really is. In times of great need, we can still experience peace, hope, and joy because our God *is* God.

His peace is incomprehensible and unexplainable, but it's incredibly real. When we find ourselves at the point of greatest need, God offers His supernatural peace—something Scripture says we can barely fathom. Paul wrote, "And the peace of God, *which transcends all understanding*, will guard your hearts and your minds in Christ Jesus" (Philippians 4:7, emphasis added). To find such peace we must run to Jesus. The Bible says we are to "yoke" ourselves with Him: "Come to me, all you who are weary and burdened, and I will give you rest. Take my yoke upon you and learn from me, for I am gentle and humble in heart, and you will find rest for your souls. For my yoke is easy and my burden is light" (Matthew 11:28–30). When we are "yoked" with Christ, our hope is not limited by circumstance; our hope is not in favorable situations. Rather, our hope is in our Lord (Psalm 62:5). No matter the pain or how deep the hurt, we can come to Jesus and connect with Him; He will help us deal with our trials. He wants us to share our burdens. As we learn from Him, He will change us and return hope to our hurting hearts. This hope will hold us securely through all the harsh realities of this life.

When our eyes are turned toward Him and His faithfulness, He will turn our sorrow into joy. He promises in Jeremiah 31:13, "I will turn their mourning into gladness; I will give them comfort and joy instead of sorrow." Our God will bring bright, new mornings into our darkest nights. He is faithful to fill our weary souls with His peace, hope, and joy. Sadly, this won't wipe away all our pain during times of trial, but they make the trials along the trail bearable and enable us to keep climbing up the mountain.

Know–Be–Live

KNOW

Read Psalm 13:1–6. Notice how the passage breaks down into three parts. In verses 1–2, the psalmist questions God, asking Him, "How long?" In verses 3–4, the psalmist makes his petition, asking God for specific relief. Then, in verses 5–6, the psalmist closes his prayer with a statement of trust and praise. He doesn't wait on the Lord's answer before offering his praise and affirming his faith in a loving, good God. How might you model this type of prayer in the midst of your own suffering?

_____

_____

_____

_____

_____

BE

Read Psalm 62:5–8. What does it mean to "find rest in God"? How easy or difficult is it for you to live this out during times of pain?

_____

_____

_____

_____

_____

_____

Know–Be–Live

LIVE

Read James 1:2–12. What would it look like for you to "persevere under trial"? What steps can you take to advance your journey from trial to perseverance to maturity (verses 2–4)? Why is wisdom so important in this situation?

_____

_____

_____

_____

_____

_____

_____

_____

_____

_____

_____

_____

_____

_____

_____

_____

_____

CHAPTER 7
Strength to the Summit

<hr/>

Even to your old age and gray hairs I am he,
I am he who will sustain you.
—ISAIAH 46:4

I have always loved celebrating my birthday—and I've had quite a few! When I was a little girl, I spent the weeks before my birthday thinking about it, dreaming about, it, planning for it, and anticipating every part. I loved the gifts and the parties, of course, but I was mainly excited about simply getting older. When you're a child, you're in such a rush to grow up. When you're in elementary school, you dream about how great it'd be in middle school. When you're in middle school, you can't wait to be in high school. When you're in high school, you start dreaming about college. When you're in college, you're ready to get out to start your career and maybe get married. It can all feel like a race to some finish line we imagine in the distance, just out of reach, when our lives will be complete and we'll have all we ever wanted.

As the youngest of three children in the Cathy home, this was especially true of me. And, as one birthday melted into the next and as the years ticked by at a seemingly faster rate, I started to realize I was on board a train called aging—and that train was moving *fast!* These days, I still love my birthdays, but I wouldn't mind if the years in between slowed down a little bit. That's how it is with aging. Growing up seems so exciting when you're young. You can't wait until you have the freedom and adventure that come with being a teenager and then an adult. We seldom stop to think about where all those birthdays are taking us though. Every child I meet seems to want to grow *older*—but no child wants to grow *old*.

There are many fears and stigmas attached to aging. We worry about our health, our strength, and our resources. We worry about feeling useful and relevant in a rapidly advancing world. We worry about staying informed and intelligent in the never-ending march of technology. We worry about watching our friends and loved ones die. We worry about losing our spouses. We worry about our grown children getting busy and leaving us to go through our final years alone. Or, if our children remain involved, we worry about becoming a burden *on* them or being treated like a child *by* them. We worry about being marginalized, condescended to, and hidden away somewhere. Those are the realities you never seem to consider when you're a little child dreaming about getting older.

However, the Bible reminds us, "What has been will be again, what has been done will be done again; there is nothing new under the sun" (Ecclesiastes 1:9). That means the aged will always be relevant because we will always have the one thing our children and grandchildren lack: experience. If you're blessed to walk the earth long enough, you'll rack up a world of experience that those around you desperately need. Nineteenth-century philosopher George Santayana wrote, "Those who cannot remember the past are condemned to repeat it." As generation gives way to generation, wisdom and knowledge become the currency of our seniors. We are the ones called to share what we've learned—our mistakes and our victories—to ensure the generations behind us are equipped to climb even higher than we could. We want them to avoid our missteps and build on our successes. As we've said before, our goal should be to blaze a trail for others to follow. That only happens, though, when we're willing to follow the trail those before us left behind.

Aging is an exciting and terrifying mountain we all must climb. It is wrought with adventure, joy, danger, and rewards the young could never dream of. Fortunately, there are plenty of people at the top of the mountain shouting down tips and directions to help the rest of us make the climb. When it comes to facing the mountain of aging, I think there are three specific milestones we must all reach on the journey: learning from our elders when we're young, saying goodbye to our elders as we grow, and ultimately becoming elders ourselves as we reach the top of the mountain. Let's dig in and explore these three inevitable phases of life.

LEARNING FROM OUR ELDERS

As I grow older, I realize how blessed I've been throughout my life by the wonderful elders God's put around me. They have made such a tremendous impact on me, helping me in everything from my relationships to my marriage to my career. Watching them go through life and being the beneficiary of their wisdom and experience has saved me from falling off the mountain more times than I can count. As long as I can remember, I've been surrounded by godly men and women with decades of life experience who have graciously invested in my life in big and small ways.

FAMILY ELDERS

The most significant elder influences in my life were in my family. My four aunts on my father's side each taught me something unique. Aunt Esther, who spent most of her life in a wheelchair due to polio at birth, never let her disability slow her down mentally, emotionally, or physically. She learned to drive, wrote a book, worked as a librarian, and was a masterful storyteller. She taught me how to tell my own stories and keep a positive attitude no matter what life throws at me. Aunt Myrtle was an entrepreneur, just like my dad. She ran her own cooking and catering business, teaching me the power of hard work and a can-do attitude. Aunt Gladys owned and operated her own gift shop. She's the one who encouraged my father to open his first Chick-fil-A in Greenbriar Mall in Atlanta. She taught me to always believe in others, even when they don't believe in themselves. Finally, Aunt Agnes, a pastor's wife, worked tirelessly with her husband to spread the gospel and minister to their community. She taught me how to be effective in ministry and how to maintain a healthy partnership in marriage—and, of course, how to make the best homemade dinner rolls in the world. My

aunts blazed so many important trails up the mountain of life; I
would have been a fool to ignore the lessons they were so generously willing and ready to share with me!

Of all the elders who touched my life, though, none but my
own mother was dearer to me than my maternal grandmother,
Ida Irene McNeil, whom I will always know as Granny. I've
mentioned a few times that my mother never knew her father.
He left when my mom was an infant, and Granny remained a
single mother for the rest of her life. Rather than growing bitter
at the hard hand she was dealt, Granny embraced life and lived it
to the fullest. She was extremely healthy and active throughout
her life. She got up with the sun and faced each day with energy
and good humor. She enjoyed surrounding herself with God's
creation—working in her yard, caring for plants, and growing
the most beautiful flowers I've ever seen. We'd find her out in
the garden well after dark, toiling in the dirt and singing songs
of praise.

I never recall Granny driving a car, taking a nap, or
complaining about life. She had a modest home and lived a
simple lifestyle. She wasn't concerned with the stuff she didn't
have; she was more concerned with loving God and loving people.
She was humble, quiet, kind, and reserved. She unashamedly
lived out her faith in front of everyone, and she taught us to
do the same. Above all, she taught us the importance of serving
other people with love, using her talents as a professional seam-
stress, caring for God's creation, and valuing family. I would
not be who I am today if it weren't for my grandmother. She
climbed a mountain I can't imagine—being a single mother in
the 1920s and 1930s—but she never lost her footing. Granny
never knew the impact she would have on her grandchildren,
great-grandchildren, and great-great-grandchildren but her
faith and resolve live on today in and through the people I love
the most. She didn't just *reach* the summit—she danced on it.

ELDERS ALL AROUND

My brothers and I spent a lot of time in our father's first restaurant when we were young. Dad operated a nice little place called the Dwarf House in Hapeville, Georgia. We spent many afternoons there working on homework, helping with chores, and, I suspect, getting in the way of the employees. However, they never complained about us being around. In fact, they did just the opposite: they spent time with us. These hard-working grownups encouraged us to behave, work hard, and be kind. We saw them practice what they preached, too, as they demonstrated remarkable loyalty and commitment to our family and our customers.

I remember so many of those people who practically raised us every afternoon after school. They helped shape our lives and demonstrated a strong work ethic. One day, a server named Zelma strapped a white apron on me, hiked it up to my armpits so it wouldn't drag the floor, put me up on a stool, and taught me the perfect way to top a lemon pie. Another server, Betty, often gave me a pad and pencil and had me write down customers' orders for her. Of course, I was so young I couldn't write very well, so Betty had to hover within earshot to make sure we got the order right. I'm sure including me made her job a little harder, but she didn't mind. She was happy to give me something to do to boost my confidence and make me feel useful. Some days, at my mother's prompting, my brothers and I would dress up as dwarves from Snow White—in homemade costumes made by Granny, no less— and sing for the restaurant patrons. As we got older, we took on more serious duties like restocking the displays, picking up trash in the parking lot, and taking orders (for real this time). These weren't always glamorous times, but they are special memories. I owe a tremendous debt of gratitude to those older men and women. They not only demonstrated extreme patience with the three little children running around their workplace, but they chose to make those hours count by investing into us so heavily.

Although my father and his employees took the business side of the restaurant seriously, it was never simply a *job* for those who worked there—it was a *family*. Everyone there—the manager, servers, and cooks—did their jobs with a smile on their faces. They actually liked being together, and they were serious about providing an excellent experience for every customer. In fact, they extended their family atmosphere to everyone who walked in the door, which no doubt contributed to the Dwarf House's success and stellar reputation. Everyone who worked there demonstrated what it means to "serve one another humbly in love" (Galatians 5:13). While every customer was treated as an honored guest at the Dwarf House, I watched how the employees gave special reverence to the older ones. There was an air of respect to the way the restaurant staff spoke to and served them. Those lessons—watching how my elders treated me *and* how they treated older customers—shaped my experience at a critical time in my youth. I'm sure that's why I have such high esteem for my elders today.

ELDER MENTORS

In every season of life, during every mountain of adversity, I can honestly say that God ensured I would not climb alone. No matter where John and I have lived, the Lord has been faithful to provide wise, loving mentors. When we were in college, God sent us Kathryn Giers, a pastor's widow we knew from church. Despite the age difference, I immediately *clicked* with Mrs. Giers. We became great friends, and John and I made a habit out of taking her out for pizza (her favorite) after church every Sunday night. Kathryn never had children of her own, but she threw her arms open to John and me, investing in us as much as any relative ever could. She showed us how to grow old gracefully, influence younger generations, love the church, treasure God's Word, and make the most out of marriage. Although we never knew her late husband, we felt as though we did because of the loving way she always spoke of him.

She was such a powerful figure in our lives that we chose to honor her by naming one of our daughters, Joy Kathryn, after her.

Even in Brazil, God continually surrounded us with older men and women who would become friends and mentors. Bill and Jerry Ichter, Bill and Barbara Moseley, Orman and Elizabeth Gwynn—I could go on and on about the people who seemed to appear just when we needed them the most. They became our friends and, in many ways, our surrogate parents and grandparents while our real family was half a world away. In each case, these mentors came alongside us and helped us carry our load. They had already journeyed further than we had, and they were always willing to share their wisdom and experience.

By opening my heart to what these great mentors—family members and friends alike—had learned and paying attention to the choices they had made, I was able to take a few shortcuts in my own climb. They pointed out danger zones I was able to avoid and offer suggestions on better routes to take along the way. Their influence has been an unmistakable blessing in my life, impacting not only me but also my husband, children, grandchildren, employees, friends, and thousands of students who have participated in camps I've led. They taught me that my experience doesn't have to be mine *alone*. I can incorporate what others have learned into my experience and, more importantly, I can share what I have learned with others. When you come to view your life through that lens, you discover that you're standing in a river of experiences. Each one flows right into the next. And, when you realize there are other people in the river with you, you begin to notice how someone's experiences upstream can shape and change yours. In return, you see that your own experiences flow out of you and can impact those coming up from behind. That's the power of elder relationships. There's a world of wisdom and knowledge all around us; we just have to be willing to look.

SAYING GOODBYE TO OUR ELDERS

If there is one major downside to spending time with and learning from older people, it's that you will eventually have to say goodbye to them one last time. We will discuss grief in detail in the following chapter; for now, though, I'd very much like to tell you about my mother. I've already shared several fun stories about my childhood, but now I want to invite you into my experiences with Mom in the last chapters of her life. By sharing my own recent experiences, perhaps I can challenge you to make the most of whatever time you have left with the elders you most treasure.

I moved out of state from my parents when I started college at age eighteen. There, I opened a Chick-fil-A restaurant, met my husband, got married, graduated, and started raising a family. Later, John and I moved the family to Brazil for ten years. By the time we returned home from the mission field, I had lived far away from my parents for almost thirty years. Life came full circle when, in August of 2003, we moved next door to Mom and Dad and later built a house on the family farm. They were both in their eighties at the time, but their health was strong. I took full advantage of every possible moment to make up for our many years apart, spending as much time with them as I could.

I often checked in on Mom while Dad was at work and usually found her busy at some pursuit. I've said before that she was always learning some new trick or trade, such as how to fix the plumbing, repair the dishwasher, and use a computer. Because we lived far out in the country and Dad was busy at work, Mom learned how to do just about anything that needed to be done. She'd say, "I couldn't get a repairman out here for love or money, so I learned to do things myself."

Mom challenged herself to grow orchids and become an expert at oil painting. To maximize her time and continue learning, she listened to audiobooks, business lectures, sermons, and motivational speakers as she worked around the house. She enjoyed music, art, flowers, and her church. For thirty years, she taught Bible study classes for thirteen-year-old girls. She loved her husband and family. She treasured her relationship with Jesus above everything else. Through her philanthropic pursuits, she touched the lives of thousands of families and children who may never know the debt they owe to her. She truly left her mark on the world.

As Mom and Dad grew older and needed more help, I realized Mom had already taught me everything I needed to know about caring for aging parents. She had done an amazing job taking care of her own mother, my precious Granny, in the final years of her life. Now I realized it was my turn—and I was determined to live up to the fine example Mom set for me. When she stopped driving, I began taking her everywhere she needed to go. We spent so much time in the car driving to doctor appointments, the hair salon, the grocery store, and so on. I sat with her every week to organize her medications, and I helped her with her wardrobe by matching tops with pants in her closet. What many may see as a chore, I saw as a tremendous blessing. I loved every minute I spent laughing and crying with her during those years. I may not have realized it at the time, but God gave me a beautiful gift: the gift of time and conversation. I feel like I got to know my mother better in those final few years than I did all the years before. She would challenge me with what she was learning from the Bible and her walk with the Lord. I would try to encourage her to remain strong because of her influence on our family. She would often talk out loud to her heavenly Father while getting dressed or riding in the car with me. Whenever it happened, I smiled on the inside. What a blessing to watch her grow old with grace.

Mom never lost her zest for life. I once visited her "80s and Up" Sunday School class when Mom was about eighty-nine. She announced to the ladies in the class, "Just because you're getting old doesn't mean you have to dress the part!" Then she lifted the hem of her modest dress ever so slightly to reveal the bright red slip underneath. My mother always maintained a youthful mind and promoted positive thinking everywhere she went. On rainy days, she put on the brightest thing she had to wear and never used a black umbrella. She preferred one that was hot pink, bold blue, or even polka dotted! Mom was sunshine to many people, especially on dark, dreary days.

She was different things to different people. To Dad, she was his nurturer and partner for almost sixty-six years. She was at his side at every turn, turning that little Dwarf House restaurant into a leading national brand. To her children, she was the number-one cheerleader and encourager, always pointing us to Christ and reminding us *who* we were and *whose* we were. To her grandchildren and great-grandchildren, she was a relentless prayer warrior and spiritual mentor. To her friends, she was true and loyal, using her unique gifts to serve them generously. To the rest of the world, including you, she was the one to stand on top of the mountain and proclaim, "You can—*with God*!" She was a constant, living reminder of Paul's words, "I can do all things through Christ who strengthens me" (Philippians 4:13, NKJV).

Mom's legacy can be summed up in the Know–Be–Live model we've used throughout this book. Her life is a challenge to the coming generations to *know* Jesus more deeply, *be* transformed in their character, and *live* a life of kingdom influence. That's what she taught me, and that's the mark she left on the world. Saying goodbye to her was more difficult than I can describe, but I still rejoice in the life she lived—and I thank God for bringing me home in time to walk beside her every day for the last decade of her life.

Reaching the Summit: Becoming Elders Ourselves

Once you reach the age when your older friends, family members, and mentors start passing away, you realize something that shouldn't be shocking (but often is): you're getting older. I'm in my early sixties as I write this book. I remember a time when "sixty" sounded so old! But I don't feel old at all. I still have an active, often busy lifestyle. John and I still go out on dates and socialize just like we did when we were much younger. I get on the floor and play with my grandchildren just like I played with their parents thirty years ago. I travel for business, exercise, volunteer at camps, and enjoy speaking engagements across the country. I'm the same Trudy I've always been; I just have a few more wrinkles and a few more years of experience and memories than I used to.

Our usefulness is not measured by how fast we step but by how high we climb.

I've been blessed with relatively good health so far, but I've had several friends whose progression into their senior years hasn't been as smooth. They've struggled with health, memories, and independence. More often than that, though, they struggle with significance. This is something we all face from time to time, worrying that the world has sped up too much and we'll never catch up to it. That's what makes aging such a particularly frightening mountain. It looms before all of us, and we know the climb will be a challenge. However, we fear we won't have the strength to reach the summit by the time we get there. As the challenges of old age begin to overtake us, we may become tempted to give up, sit down, relax, and quietly fade away. I can't speak for you, but that's not the way I've lived my life up to this point, and it's not the way I want to live the life ahead.

Psalm 92:14 assures us that we will "still bear fruit in old age" and that we "will stay fresh and green." It doesn't matter how old you are, what you've been through, or what mountain you're facing. I refuse to believe that my best years are behind me. I strive to make every year better than the year before. That's how you get to the summit, by climbing over your past failures and moving beyond your past successes. Each experience builds on the previous one; that means the longer you live, the more experiences you have to take you higher and higher!

Our usefulness is not measured by how fast we step but by how high we climb. Even as age slows us down, sometimes frustratingly so, our lives can still be vivid examples of what it means to live, move, and breathe in Jesus. Age does not diminish our call to be His ambassadors in a dark world. The fruit of the spirit doesn't dry up because the branches show a little more wear and tear. As long as we draw breath, every moment is an opportunity to create a greater legacy for those we will one day leave behind. The mountain of aging is not a depressing or impossible mountain to climb; rather, it can be the most rewarding summit of our lives.

NOTHING NEW UNDER THE SUN

At the start of this chapter, we read Scripture's view of aging: "What has been will be again, what has been done will be done again; there is nothing new under the sun" (Ecclesiastes 1:9). The pressures the modern Millennial feels aren't so different from what the Baby Boomers went through. The temptations today's teens experience existed for their grandparents. Sure, technology changes and society advances, but are all those innovations actually making us happier and healthier than previous generations? Sadly, that doesn't seem to be the case. Study after study shows the current generation of adults to be the most stressed, anxious, and generally unhappy in history. More Americans are prescribed medications to treat depression than ever before. If this is true, then why on earth are we not paying more attention to the wisdom and experience of those who have already faced and overcome the challenges in our way? We have so much to learn from them if we're only willing to listen.

In His perfect wisdom, God ensured that several generations would live and work together in every part of the world. No matter where on earth you go, you'll find children, teens, young adults, the middle-aged, and the elderly. In many parts of the world, you'll routinely see three or four generations under one roof! I don't believe that's an accident. I think God knew we'd need the benefit of our elders' experiences, so He made sure there were plenty of elders around. Only together can the generations present a complete picture of what love is meant to be: a hand outstretched toward others in service, encouragement, and love. As the great Marcus Tullius Cicero so perfectly summarized, "Nature has but a single path and you travel it only once. Each stage of life has its own appropriate qualities—weakness in childhood, boldness in youth, seriousness in middle age, and maturity in old age. These are the fruits that must be harvested in due season." As we reach the summit of the mountain of life, I pray you will always strive to harvest those precious fruits of experience from everyone around you, young and old.

Know–Be–Live

KNOW

Benjamin Franklin said, "Those who love deeply never grow old; they may die of old age, but they die young." What biblical wisdom is reflected in Franklin's wise observation? Cite a few Bible passages and explain how they relate.

_____

_____

_____

_____

_____

_____

BE

Read Psalm 92:12–14. What does it mean to you to "still bear fruit in old age" and to "stay fresh and green"? What fruit are you bearing now (regardless of your age), and how might that fruit continue to flourish as you get older?

_____

_____

_____

_____

_____

Know—Be—Live

LIVE

What opportunities and unique experiences has God given you for you to share with another generation? How can you make the most of those opportunities? Be specific, outlining at least three ways you can pass your wisdom onto others.

CHAPTER 8

Anchored Securely

When you pass through the waters, I will be with you;
and when you pass through the rivers, they will not sweep
over you. When you walk through the fire, you will not be
burned; the flames will not set you ablaze.

—Isaiah 43:2

Life is tough. It hurts sometimes. In fact, it hurts *a lot* of the time. Though we serve a perfect God, we don't live in a perfect world. People aren't perfect. Marriages aren't perfect. Our bodies aren't perfect. There are no perfect parents, perfect jobs, perfect homes, perfect friendships. In short, there's no perfect life. We're flawed people living in a flawed world, and that means we're going to go through some hard times. We've talked about that and we've seen that Jesus promised trouble in this world (John 16:33). Isaiah prophesied the same thing. In Isaiah 43:2, found at the beginning of this chapter, the prophet says, "*When* you pass through the waters . . . *when* you pass through the rivers . . . *when* you walk through the fire" (emphasis added). He never says *if*; it's always *when*. Bottom line: trouble is coming.

No matter who we are, how much we have, or where we come from, we've all felt the pain of loss. We've all been touched by grief. From our earliest days, we've known the sting of losing something of great importance—a lost pacifier, a special blanky, a favorite toy. As we grow a bit older, the losses seem bigger; losing an important ball game or the death of a beloved pet can shake us to the core. As we enter adulthood, the stakes get higher; a profound loss can rip the earth from under our feet. The loss of a relationship, job, dream, or reputation can bring us to the point of despair. Physical sickness can throw us into a state of hopelessness. The loss of a loved one can make us question everything we believe. The devastation of divorce can make us wonder if life is little more than a cruel joke.

Are you feeling encouraged yet? I know these are hard things to think about, but it's real life. These are things we all go through; none of us is immune to the aches and pains of life on earth. No one is too rich to avoid loss. No one is "too blessed to be stressed" *all the time*. Of course, I can't know what you're going through as you read this book. At this very moment, you may be asking yourself, *Is it really possible for God to bless a broken heart?* You may wonder, *Can I really scale and conquer the mountains of loss in my life?* Or, more to the point, you may be haunted by the question, *How do I climb this mountain of loss without losing my faith?* First, I want to say that I understand. I've shared many devastating losses and struggles in this book, and I'll share a few more in this chapter. Again, none of us is immune. Second, let me assure you that God is bigger than any mountain you face. His love soars higher than the pinnacle of your pain and flows deeper than the ocean of your sorrow. He is your anchor.

Romans 8:38–39 says, "For I am convinced that neither death nor life, neither angels nor demons, neither the present nor the future, nor any powers, neither height nor depth, nor anything else in all creation, will be able to separate us from the love of God that is in Christ Jesus our Lord." God's love remains. Even when we are blinded by loss, He is there. When life grows dark, He is there. When the future looks bleak, He stands close, ready to embrace you the moment you turn to Him. The Lord will lift you up when you find yourself in the pits of despair and set your feet on solid rock when the ground under you turns into quicksand. No matter how wounded your heart, your God is Yahweh, the God who is always there. No matter how alone you feel, your God is El Roi, the Lord who sees. When you feel hopeless, Abba, your loving heavenly Father, will hold you close. When you are lost in the darkness of your pain, Yahweh Raah, your Shepherd, will find you. Your God is Yahweh Rapha, the Lord who heals. He is Yahweh Jirah, the One who provides. He is Yahweh Shalom, the One who brings you peace.

God doesn't *shield* us from pain and loss. Rather, He *walks with us* through pain and loss. As I've gotten older and suffered through many dark days and painful goodbyes, I've discovered that God anchors us securely as He walks us through three phases of grief:

1.   Facing loss.
2.   Processing through the pain.
3.   Finding purpose in grief.

I'll never tell you the process is easy, and I'll offer no quick solutions to your pain, but I believe we can see God move as we explore these three levels of the climb through grief.

FACING LOSS

Whatever grief you face throughout your life, the Bible makes God's response crystal clear. Jesus said, "Blessed are those who mourn for they shall be comforted" (Matthew 5:4). That may sound like a fantasy when you're dreading an impending loss, but I experienced the truth of Jesus's promise when I lost my mother.

Mom's death was not totally unexpected. Dad had died less than a year earlier, she was ninety-two years old, and she'd been hospitalized for ongoing heart problems. We knew it was coming. We were as prepared as anyone could be. But then, one day, she was gone. The preparation didn't seem to matter when I heard her take her last breath. The loss overwhelmed me. I couldn't escape it; it clung to me. I cried every day for weeks. When others offered words of comfort, I cried. When I went to bed at night and knew I could no longer call her to say goodnight, I cried. When I thought about stopping by her house to visit her, as I had done almost daily for the past twelve years, I cried. As I sifted through the things she left behind in her home and recalled cherished memories, I cried. It was as though every thought, every action, every feeling was taken captive by the grief I felt. I had gone through much of this when my father died, of course, but this time was different. This time, I realized *both* my parents were gone. I was almost sixty years old, but I felt like an orphaned child.

Grief is a natural response to loss. As Scripture says, "There is a time for everything, and a season for every activity under the heavens . . . there is a time to weep and a time to laugh, a time to mourn and a time to dance" (Ecclesiastes 3:1–4). I believe grief isn't just a *natural* response; I think it is the *essential* response. It is nothing to be ashamed of, ignore, deny, or try to speed through. My mother's death made grief clear to me in a powerfully new way. I realized, maybe for the first time, that grief is *real*—and our reaction to grief must be real, as well. We can't fake our way through it or lie to ourselves and others about what we're feeling. You can't climb the mountain if you pretend it's a molehill.

GRIEVING MORE THAN DEATH

While losing a cherished family member or friend is one of the most crushing blows we can experience in this life, it's not the only loss we'll feel. We're often blindsided by all kinds of loss from every part of our lives. Losing a job, going through a divorce, moving to a new

---

YOU CAN'T CLIMB THE MOUNTAIN
IF YOU PRETEND IT'S A MOLEHILL.

---

city, dealing with an illness, worrying about a sick child, moving from one life stage to another—all these things and more create many of the same feelings as a significant death. Many people resist calling these things seasons of grief, but that's a huge mistake. *Grief* is absolutely the best word to describe what we experience when a significant part of our lives is ripped away. Refusing to call it by name only delays the healing process we desperately need.

This was the case for me when, after thirteen years, I stepped aside from my role as Director of WinShape Camps for Girls. After much prayer and counsel, I knew the time had come and the Lord was calling me to a different path. Moving on from this position was a tremendous loss for me. I was releasing a significant leadership position, relationships, and unique opportunities of influence. The sadness and mourning were very real. This was *grief* in every sense of the word.

Rather than suppressing that sadness, I've tried to focus on the joys of that season as I embrace the challenges of this new phase of life. My husband won't hesitate to attest that the adjustment has not been easy for me. I've struggled with a sense of purpose and usefulness, and I've come to realize that I had tied much of my significance to the position I held. In many ways, *who I was* and *what I did* had become a jumbled mess—one that I'm still trying to untangle. If you've been through a major job change or have retired from a career you were passionate about, you probably know what I mean. These unexpected emotions and realizations have challenged me to take a good look at who I really am as I climb this new mountain.

Grief—and recognizing grief—is an essential part of a healthy, mature life. Loss brings change, and that's usually scary. Most of us don't like change; we often try to avoid it at all costs. Yet change is

---

CHANGE BRINGS GROWTH,
AND IF WE AREN'T GROWING, WE'RE DYING.

---

one of life's constants—it will come, no matter how much we try to keep the status quo. That's a good thing. Change brings growth, and if we aren't growing, we're dying. Consider children. Parents may hate seeing their tiny babies grow up, but how terrible would it be if our little ones never grew, never matured, and never experienced the blessings of living a rich life in Christ? The only thing I love more than the memory of my four little children running around the house is seeing the fine men and women they've become. And a child's growth is not without pain, is it? Babies cut teeth, but no one would say that pain isn't worth the benefit. Teenagers ache from growing pains, but that's a small price to pay for a healthy adult body. Though it comes through tears, pain usually indicates the end of one climb and the beginning of another—and every climb takes you closer to the summit.

PROCESSING THROUGH THE PAIN

When we're suffering through the throes of heartbreak, it can be hard to see the "comfort" Jesus promised in Matthew 5:4. We can come to view grief as an obstacle, but I think that's the wrong view. Instead of seeing grief as a problem that must be solved, I prefer to see it as a process that must be worked through. That grief is taking us somewhere; it's leading us to a changed life. If we overlook this fact or willfully choose to ignore it, we can end up stuck. You've seen people who are stuck in their grief, haven't you? It may be years or even decades since they experienced a significant loss, but you can tell the pain is as fresh today as it was then. You can also see that their lives haven't moved beyond what's now a years-old tragedy. That's because they've been unable to process through the pain. As we work through our grief, and as I continue to learn new things through the losses I've experienced (and continue to experience), I want to share four ways people tend to process their pain: by repressing it, by putting it in God's hands, by finding a purpose in it, and by using it as fuel to help others. Let's quickly look at each.

REPRESSING GRIEF

Through much trial, error, and experience over the years, I have learned that grief demands openness. That can come in the form of talking to a friend, working with a counselor, or simply being honest about your pain with God. However and to whomever you choose to open up, you've *got* to give a voice to your anguish. There have been times in my life when I've refused to do so, when I've tried to bury the heartache underneath my work, my relationships, and general busyness. Every single time I've tried that, it has blown up in my face. When I hold in my pain, I risk becoming an unpredictable, ticking timebomb. My mood changes, my attitude gets out of whack, my patience disappears, my enjoyment of life becomes a memory. The pain I've tried to bury deep within myself starts seeping through the cracks as the pressure builds. Eventually, that bomb goes off. All that pain and grief and frustration and rage comes out who-knows-how on who-knows-who when I'm who-knows-where. I end up experiencing more pain—and *causing* more pain—because I foolishly tried to repress what I was feeling. It just never works.

THE FIRST STEP TOWARD RESTORATION, THEN, IS TO ADMIT THAT YOU'RE BROKEN.

We never quite get over the pain of loss, but it is necessary to process through the pain. Holding onto yesterday's sorrow prevents me from moving forward toward my future. When we choose to wallow in our grief, we set a course of agony that will keep our feet planted firmly in the past. We're literally trading tomorrow's joy for yesterday's sorrow. That's a bad trade. I know how hard it is. I've been there many times, and I've walked with friends who have tried to live in denial, refusing to experience the full weight of their grief. But I've never seen anyone—myself included—make it the summit by refusing to climb. The first step toward restoration, then, is to admit that you're broken.

TRUSTING GOD WITH YOUR GRIEF

How we respond to loss can affect the rest of our lives. God doesn't want us to carry that burden alone. He has given us His Son, His Word, and His Holy Spirit to carry us through our darkest days. Jesus calls, "Come to me, all you who are weary and burdened, and I will give you rest" (Matthew 11:28). Over and over again, Scripture reminds us that we are children of a loving God, and our heavenly Father wants us to place our grief in His hands. Here are just a few of His promises:

"The LORD *is close to the brokenhearted and saves those who are crushed in spirit."* (PSALM 34:18)

"Never will I leave you; never will I forsake you." (HEBREWS 13:5)

"Even though I walk through the darkest valley, I will fear no evil, for you are with me; your rod and your staff, they comfort me." (PSALM 23:4)

"Peace I leave with you; my peace I give you. I do not give to you as the world gives. Do not let your hearts be troubled and do not be afraid." (JOHN 14:27)

"Shout for joy, you heavens; rejoice, you earth; burst into song, you mountains! For the LORD *comforts his people and will have compassion on his afflicted ones."* (ISAIAH 49:13)

"Humble yourselves, therefore, under God's mighty hand, that he may lift you up in due time. Cast all your anxiety on him because he cares for you." (1 PETER 5:6–7)

"Praise be to the God and Father of our Lord Jesus Christ, the Father of compassion and the God of all comfort, who comforts us in all our troubles, so that we can comfort those in any trouble with the comfort we ourselves receive from God. For just as we share abundantly in the sufferings of Christ, so also our comfort abounds through Christ." (2 CORINTHIANS 1:3–5)

These are only a few of the assurances we have in God's Word that He will be close to those who grieve. He stands ready to wrap His love around our hurting hearts.

That image makes me think of my grandchildren. They like to play rough, and bumps, bruises, and skinned knees abound whenever they're together. When the inevitable accident happens, I can predict with certainty what will happen next. No matter which grownup is present when the injury occurs—even if I, their doting grandmother, stand right in front of the injured child with my arms open wide— there's practically no chance that child will run to me. In fact, they'll run right past me and into the open arms of their mother. That's where they find security and comfort like nowhere else.

When life skins my knee (or breaks my heart), I have a heavenly Father standing by, always within reach, just waiting for me to run to Him. Oftentimes, though, God is the *last* One we want to run to. Sometimes, we even run *away* from Him when we're

---

LIKE A CHILD WONDERING WHY HIS MOTHER WASN'T THERE TO CATCH HIM WHEN HE FELL, WE BLAME GOD FOR NOT PROTECTING US FROM THE THING THAT CAUSED SO MUCH PAIN.

---

hurting. Like a child wondering why his mother wasn't there to catch him when he fell, we blame God for not protecting us from the thing that caused so much pain. That sends us off in the wrong direction. It leaves us stuck on the side of the mountain or, worse, sends us falling back down it.

I pray that you can find a way to trust God with your pain. It is in His presence that I find comfort for my hurting soul and healing for my battered heart. He is my perfect, loving Father. When I fall down, I always want to pop back up looking for where He is. When I'm inclined to run, I want to run *toward* Him and into His arms. He's the Creator of the universe, but He's not too distant to feel my pain, dry my tears, and put my feet back under me. Whatever the source of our sorrow, He holds the keys to our comfort and restoration. Does that make it easy? Does that make it hurt less or instantly make us feel better? No. Again, pain is a process. God isn't there to shield us from that process; He's there to guide us through it.

FINDING PURPOSE IN OUR PAIN

One of the most beautiful things that happens when we pour our hearts out to God is the way He will enable us to find meaning and purpose in our pain. God never wastes a hurt or experience in our lives. If we are willing, God can use our pain to help others. I would never have chosen to walk through the losses and pains I've experienced, but once on the other side of them, I am able to help others who find themselves in the middle of that same pain. Sometimes our greatest ministry comes out of our deepest hurt. Our adversity and difficulty give us credibility to help others.

SOMETIMES OUR GREATEST MINISTRY
COMES OUT OF OUR DEEPEST HURT.

In so many ways, God has used loss and pain to develop my character and make me more like Him. For example, I felt the deep grief of loss when God called us to leave our American lives behind and move to Brazil. My pain was multiplied by attempting to adjust to a totally foreign culture; I was nearly undone by my inability to speak the language. Learning Portuguese was extremely difficult for me, but our four-year-old daughter Joy picked it up easily. I became quite dependent on her to help me communicate, especially when shopping. When I did not know what to say, she would tell me the Portuguese words and I would repeat them exactly. I came to depend on her so much in this role that I sometimes forgot how young and playful she was—until that day she reminded me.

During one shopping trip, I asked Joy how to say a particular word. Seeing her chance to have a little fun with me, she invented a Portuguese word on the spot. She was so convincing! As always, she sounded it out for me, and I repeated it exactly to the sales clerk. The lady behind the counter looked at me with a puzzled expression, and then a smile broke out across her face. She looked down at Joy, who had just started to giggle, and the two shared a laugh at my expense. When I realized what Joy had done—and that I had fallen for it—I was a weird mix of frustrated, angry, and (mostly) embarrassed. I took Joy by the hand, led her back to the car, and drove home in silence. The little prankster had no way of knowing that she had just brought me to my breaking point.

When we got home, I went to my room and unleashed a tirade of pent-up frustration onto God. I told Him how much I disliked Brazil. I complained that I couldn't learn the language. I bemoaned the fact that my own daughter had taken advantage of my inability to communicate with the locals. I cried out to God, "I can't do this anymore!" Then there was quiet. The next thing I heard was not an audible voice but a clear message from the Lord. He said, "Good, Trudy. Now that you realize *you* can't do this, perhaps you'll let *Me* do it through you." At that moment, I heard my mother's voice ringing in my head, "You can—*with God*." Now that God finally had my full attention and dependence, I was ready to reclaim Luke 1:37 as my declaration of faith: "With God nothing will be impossible" (NKJV).

God used this very painful situation to teach me truth and develop my character. He took what I perceived as bad and used it for good. This seemingly small event has served to help me in many more situations of life; through it, I've learned my dependency is on the Lord and not on myself or other people.

HELPING OTHERS IN PAIN

Most of us will, several times through our lives, find ourselves helping a loved one through a time of intense pain. Maybe you've already walked a friend through a painful divorce or held someone's hand at their spouse's funeral. There are many times when we simply do not know what to do or say and yet our heart longs to show them the love of Christ in some significant way. I won't presume to be a professional counselor, but I have picked up a few important tips of what *not* to do as I've ministered to others during times of distress. As you seek to love the hurting people in your life:

- **Don't minimize their pain.** Never tell someone they shouldn't be feeling what they're feeling or say something like, "This will seem so insignificant one day." Those words aren't helpful; they can actually come across as judgmental. Someone in pain may mistake your attempt at comfort as cluelessness at best or as an insult at worst.
- **Don't offer easy solutions or trite platitudes.** Here's a tip: If you feel a cliché coming out of your mouth when you're trying to comfort someone, shut it down quickly. And if you're inclined to say anything that starts with, "All you need to do is . . ." or "You just have to . . .," then please stop talking. There are no easy solutions to pain.
- **Don't tell them they should be grateful.** Pastor Charles Stanley often talks about the pain of losing his dear mother. Even though he was sixty years old at the time, the loss was extremely painful to him as a son. He later wrote, "The emotional wound was deep and hurt for many months. When well-meaning friends remarked, 'We're so happy your mom is in heaven!' I became angry. Without their realizing it, they were trying to short-circuit my grief."[9] I could not agree more. When my own mother died, I didn't need to hear someone tell me how blessed I was to know I'll see her again in heaven; I needed someone to hold me quietly as I wept.

9   Charles F. Stanley, "Understanding Grief," In Touch Ministries, July 28, 2014, https://www.intouch.org/read/understanding-grief.

- **Don't try to fill the silence.** Your friend's pain is not a problem for you to fix. If you feel the urge to fill the silence as you sit with them, you'll probably end up breaking one of the rules above by mistake. It's okay to be quiet. They probably don't need your wisdom; they need *you*.

Again, I'm not a professional counselor, but I've seen many well-meaning friends fall into some (or all) of these traps. All of these can be avoided, though, by simply showing up and being present for your friend. The most powerful message you can share is often the one that needs no words. Don't try to *tell* someone how much you love them; just *show* them. Be there for them. Put an arm around them and let them cry in silence. Go cut their yard for them or take them a meal without being asked. You're their friend; you already have permission to serve them!

FINDING HOPE IN HEARTACHE

Three days after my mother's death, I had the privilege of speaking at her memorial service. I stood before friends and family who had come to offer their support in our time of sorrow and loss. These were the opening words I shared:

> When I woke up this morning, the first thing I thought about was my grief. Our family is grieving the loss of a mother, grandmother, and great-grandmother. But what I want you to know today is that we do not grieve as those without hope, for to be absent from the body is to be present with the Lord (1 Thessalonians 4:13; 2 Corinthians 5:8). Mother always told me this day would surely come, and it did. She assured me she would not live forever. Her one request for this service today was that it would be all about her Father, her heavenly Father.

That was one of the hardest days of my life, but we clung to the promise of comfort Jesus gave us so long ago (Matthew 5:4).

Months later, I found myself rereading the brief description of Anna in Luke 2:36–38: "There was also a prophet, Anna, the daughter of Phanuel, of the tribe of Asher. She was very old; she had lived with her husband seven years after her marriage, and then was a widow until she was eighty-four. She never left the temple but worshiped night and day, fasting and praying." That is literally everything we know about Anna, and yet it is enough for us to get a glimpse of her character. She had been a widow most of her life. She had experienced tragic loss and known deep sorrow. Anna could have opted to be hard, bitter, resentful, and rebellious against God. Instead, she chose to let those circumstances make her more in tune with the heart of God. At the advanced age of eighty-four, she had still never ceased to hope.

Age can take away bodily energy and strength. It can also cause hearts to grow so weary of the uphill journey that cherished hopes are allowed to die. But Anna seemed to keep her feet on the path, determined to climb every mountain, no matter how great. It seems she learned to lift her eyes up to the mountains to find her anchor and strength in the Lord who made heaven and earth (Psalm 121:1). We know from Scripture that Anna never ceased to worship her God. She spent her life in His house with His people, and she was known by the community as a prayer warrior. Anna's life was filled with unshakable hope because, day after day, she stayed close to the One who was the source of her strength and in whose strength her weakness was made perfect (2 Corinthians 12:9).

So much about Anna reminds me of my mother. Mom's life was not lived in the spotlight and she did not have a platform of power, but her life continues to speak about faithfulness, kindness, gentleness, and hope. Just like Anna, Mom chose to continue the climb up life's mountains until she reached the home she so desired. She now lives in the very presence of her Lord, her "perfect Father."

Trudy's childhood home on the farm where she grew up with her two brothers climbing pine trees, riding Shetland ponies, and playing with pets including dogs, a cat, ducks, a parrot, and even a squirrel monkey.

Trudy's "second home" where she spent many hours in the kitchen with employees and customers of her father's first restaurant, the Dwarf House, which opened in Hapeville, GA, on the south side of Atlanta in 1946.

From the time she was a baby in arms, Trudy attended church weekly with her family, Jeannette, Truett, Dan, Bubba, and Trudy (left to right). Through the spiritual nurturing of her parents and exposure to the truth of God's Word, Trudy became a follower of Jesus at the age of 7.

Trudy attending the Symbol of Success Celebration at the annual Chick-fil-A Seminar in 2003 with her brother Bubba (left), Truett Cathy (father), Jeannette (mother), and older brother Dan (right).